Wow! *Stepping Out* is a powerful and poignant book, especially for REAL women in today's REAL world!

Deb Burma gives no excuses as she struggles, stretches, and strives to STEP OUT and openly shares her inner soul. All the while, she works her way to the edge with fear and trepidation. Each time, she ventures a little further with new-found confidence, trusting that God will be her life-saver. This enables her to turn her sinful obstacles into spiritual opportunities through which to share her heart and faith with those around her.

Stepping Out will give hope, healing, encouragement, and edification to be brave, to not look back with excuses for insecurities and fears. So with boldness, you can edge out on life's springboard of situations, jumping into the future with God's loving and safe arms enfolding you. What are you waiting for? You can do it!

> Terry Lee Kieschnick,
> National Speaker, Ministry Leader, Mentor

When I first heard author Deb Burma speak on this topic, it was in her keynote address for the Lutheran Women's Missionary League (LWML) convention in Peoria, Illinois, in June 2011. Prior to the convention, Deb had an unusual request: could we somehow rig up a diving board on the stage to be used in her talk. The local properties team and our audio-visual director made it happen. The theme of that convention was, "Being with Jesus—Living on the Edge."

Deb Burma has been with Jesus and in this book leads readers through the fears and struggles they face. She draws the reader into her own personal experience of fear and relates her stepping out story in the introduction and the first chapter. Sharing her vulnerability, shortcomings, and struggles, Deb's overriding message is God's grace and forgiveness in Jesus Christ. Using stories from real women, with which many are able to identify, the author draws examples from the ministry of Jesus, inviting us all to be with Jesus and learn from Him. Each chapter ends with reflection and personal applications to life, here and now.

Looking over the list of chapter titles and topics covered, I felt as if this book was written just for me. Gather a group of friends, or read this book on your own, but by all means do read it. God is inviting you to step up, dive into His Word, and step out to life on the edge.

Janice M. Wendorf,
16th President of Lutheran Women's Missionary League 2007–2011

In *Stepping Out*, Deb Burma speaks directly to a woman's heart, mind, and soul. In her conversational style, Deb highlights the self-talk that women use to avoid stepping out and taking risks. Deb is frank, and she steps out on the edge as she shares her own personal challenges, failures, and successes. How does she do it? Deb writes, "I have a Savior who enables me to keep stepping out in His strength because He keeps stepping in with His saving grace!"

This book is wonderful for one's personal reading, and it is a great book for a small-group Bible study. The questions at the end of each chapter are perfect for initiating heartfelt conversations and further Bible study. Why not step out, invite some women to your home, and start a book discussion? This is the perfect book to get you started. As a matter of fact, I plan to step out and start a book discussion at my house. Thanks, Deb, for stepping out and writing this book!

Mary E. Hilgendorf, Ph.D.,
professor emeritus, Concordia University Wisconsin

Deb Burma throws her whole self into her writing—her remarkable love for Jesus, her amazing sense of humor, her life experiences, her tender heart, and her deep understanding of God's grace toward us in Christ. These ingredients combine to create a zesty, spiritually uplifting stew that will engage, challenge, and encourage Christian women today, no matter where they find themselves along life's path. Buy and read this book! You'll be glad you did!

Jane L. Fryar, DSL,
Litt.D., Author, Educator, Speaker

Pressed, harried, worried, and stressed? *You need this book!*

Deb Burma connects with the way we live today with all its challenges and struggles—and offers courage from the Word of God, encouragement from the witness of other Christians, and a guided opportunity to reflect and grow. *You need this book!*

Step out of the darkness of holding a grudge, defending a judgmental spirit, and being a slave to perfection—into the light of God's acceptance and forgiveness. This book will lead you by the heart into God's comforting presence. *You need this book!*

Ruth N. Koch, M.A.,

NCC, Mental Health Educator

"Because Jesus steps in, we can step out," is at the heart of Deb Burma's Christ-centered and Word-weighted book *Stepping Out*. From reliance upon Jesus, born of the Holy Spirit, Deb weaves together God's inspired Word with touching accounts of Christians. She engages her readers with Jesus' forgiveness to enable them to step out from sin and Satan's traps into acts of faith only God can work. Readers will quickly recognize their own experiences in Deb's stories. They will be convicted by God's Word and lose touch with time pondering the reflections at the end of each chapter. A journey through *Stepping Out* is a trek on the path where Jesus leads. *Stepping Out* brings to mind, "For God did not give us a spirit of timidity, but a spirit of power, of love and of self-discipline" 2 Timothy 1:7.

Rev. Russell L. Sommerfeld,

Nebraska District President, LCMS

"Unsure of what steps to take to a more meaningful life? *Stepping Out* is a map to a joyous life path. Deb Burma guides the reader step-by-step away from paths of anger, fear, and insecurity and onto roads of peace, courage, and confidence. She reminds us that Jesus has already stepped toward us, ready to hold our hands on this new journey."

Sharla Fritz, speaker and author

of *Bless These Lips* and *Divine Design*

Stepping Out offers bold and inspiring encouragement to anyone desiring to step out of fear, worry, your past, or your comfort zone. Offering examples of vulnerability from personal experience, this talented author skillfully navigates readers through Scripture to offer invaluable insights and hope along with practical application. As a women's ministry leader, Deb Burma's understanding and compassion for women flows through each chapter. She knows how tough it is being a woman in this intimidating world. If you have longed to trust God wholeheartedly and embrace living life on the edge, this wisdom-packed book is a refreshing must-read.

> Donna Pyle, Speaker, Bible teacher,
> founder of Artesian Ministries,
> and author of *The God of All Comfort*

Through 1,400 shows, my listeners engaged with the experts to "step out" and follow Jesus' lead in their choices and challenges. Against this background, I applaud Deb Burma's godly counsel. Her remarkable sisterly insights free us with truth and feed our souls with hope that breaks through the yes-buts and what-ifs. Treat yourself to the secrets of edgy living by stepping out, without falling off! There's a surprising freedom connected with this read. His Edge: Your Astonishing Life... about to happen, starting with page 1!

> Phyllis Wallace, originator and host
> of "Woman to Woman" talk radio produced by
> Lutheran Hour Ministries, 1993–2011

Stepping Out

to a life on the edge

Deb Burma

CONCORDIA PUBLISHING HOUSE · SAINT LOUIS

Published by Concordia Publishing House
3558 S. Jefferson Avenue, St. Louis, MO 63118-3968
1-800-325-3040 • www.cph.org

Manufactured in the United States of America

Library of Congress Cataloging-in-Publication Data

Burma, Deb.
    Stepping out to a life on the edge / Deb Burma.
        pages cm
        ISBN 978-0-7586-3869-4
1. Christian women--Religious life. I. Title.
        BV4527.B8577 2013
        248.8'43--dc23
                                        2012050367

1 2 3 4 5 6 7 8 9 10   22 21 20 19 18 17 16 15 14 13

Table of Contents

I'd like you to use your imagination for a minute. Picture an in-ground backyard swimming pool filled with calm, clear, cool water and surrounded by a beautiful concrete patio. There's a diving board perched over the deep end. It's a hot summer day, and everyone around you is enjoying a good dunk in the shallow end of the pool. Now envision yourself standing behind the diving board on solid patio. You eye the platform, then you eagerly step up, sprint to the end, yell "Cannonball!" and jump. What awaits you is the exhilarating feeling of release and total immersion in cool, refreshing water.

Or do you?

If you have timid tootsies like mine, you stare at the diving board in front of you and wonder how you will ever move from the solid surface where your feet are firmly fastened to the slick, slippery edge w-a-y out there. Do you inch up and onto the platform, or do you remain frozen at the far end of the board, paralyzed in place? Do you focus on the fear of losing control, of being in over your head?

My stepping-out story begins with a diving board and a backyard pool, as you will read in chapter 1. Moving from behind the board, where my feet were firmly planted, stepping up and onto the spring-loaded surface, and slowly shimmying out to the edge symbolizes for me so much more than stepping away from the safety of the solid cement.

As a women's ministry leader, I love encouraging women to use the combination of their God-given abilities and their life experiences to touch others in their midst. One time in particular comes to mind. As our local congregation's ministry group was preparing for a women's retreat, I approached a friend and sister leader to ask if she would speak at the event. When I told her the topic of the speech, her mouth dropped and she exclaimed, "Did you know I have been wrestling with this very issue? Deb, who am I to minister to these women when I still struggle myself?"

You see, I *did* know that she struggled in this area. I could also see how God was increasing her faith through this issue, teaching and transforming her by His Word, guiding her by His grace, and enabling her to step out of her struggle. I knew she could address the topic biblically and personally, and that the Lord would use her to touch the hearts of many other women who shared similar issues.

I struggle with each and every topic in this book. It would be easy for me to throw my hands up in the air and exclaim, "Who am I to minister to you through these pages when I struggle so myself?" But my friend's words give me pause: *Who am I?*

I am a woman like you, a woman who wrestles with fear and worry, with pride and selfish ambition, with anger and bitterness, and with so much more.

I am a woman like you, a chosen child of God in Christ, redeemed by my Savior.

Despite my sins and shortcomings and timid tootsies, God has called me to step out of my struggles to a life on the edge. God continually covers me with His grace and fills me with His strength; He extends His hand to me, walks beside me, and empowers me to live for Him. I must admit, some days I feel as though I am taking the clichéd "one step forward and two steps back." But I have a Savior who enables me to keep stepping *out* in His strength because He keeps stepping *in* with His saving grace!

As Jesus guides me through His Word of truth, I am able to address these topics both biblically and personally, much as my friend did at the women's retreat. Through the often humorous and sometimes painful stories in every chapter of *Stepping Out,* I admit my foibles and my failures. (I'll be honest, if I had more pages, I could add more stories!)

I have the opportunity to meet with women around the country. We connect on a heart level, and many of the women I've met have shared their stories with me. While circumstances and details are different and unique, the emotional and spiritual struggles of all women are surprisingly similar. *In our sin, we all share these struggles.* Some "stepping out" stories of other women are in this book. Many are tender, others are painful, and all of them are included here to reassure you that because our Savior offers His guidance and strength, you *can* step out of your comfort zone and serve Him in whatever capacity you are called to serve. Because Christ Jesus calls you to the scary edge of living boldly as God's daughter, you can trust Him to be there with you. My hope is that these stories will speak to you personally as you relate each topic to your own life experience and will encourage you to take steps forward and plunge into a deeper faith.

Jesus takes center stage in every chapter. It is only because He steps into our lives that we can take even one tiny step toward the edge w-a-y out there. We will dive into Scripture as we examine these topics in the light of God's grace-filled Word, ever powerful and completely relevant to us today. We will look into the lives of biblical people who encountered Christ in the Gospels and consider how Jesus stepped into their lives with His great mercy and changed them forever.

The final section of each chapter is called "Life on the Edge." As we rejoice together in the Savior's work in our lives, we have the opportunity to view what life might look like beyond the foothold of struggle and w-a-y out there on the edge.

At the close of every chapter are "Reflections," questions and insights for your personal contemplation or for book club or small-group Bible study. Included in this section is the invitation to slip your feet into the sandals of someone from Scripture during their life-changing encounter with Jesus. Have a Bible handy for your reflection time.

It is my prayer that you will find great comfort in the message of God's grace in Christ, a central theme woven throughout every chapter of *Stepping Out*. As we struggle to step out of our past, our insecurity, our judgmental attitude, and other circumstances, we may be trapped into thinking, *If I just try harder* or *If I can just get my act together*. We *do* try, but on our own, we are bound to fail eventually and sink to the bottom of the pool. (Many times in my case, I fail right away.)

The world shouts, "Get a grip! Just do it already. What are you waiting for?" But our God of grace knows we cannot take even one baby step forward all by ourselves. So He comes to us right where we are, stuck in our sin, and He places His firm grip of grace upon us. Forgiven, renewed, and strengthened by the Savior, we *step out to a life on the edge,* resting in His truth, which tells us, "I can do all things through Him who strengthens me" (Philippians 4:13).

I pray also that God would work mightily in you through His Word as you apply it to your life. Allow Him to use *Stepping Out* to encourage you in your springboard to edgy living. He will lead you to take stock of your struggles and confess them to Him. And by His grace, He will unfasten your feet from where they are planted behind the diving board. He will help you step out to a place where He would have you live!

Stepping out by my Savior's strength,

Deb Burma

CHAPTER ONE

Stepping Out of My Fear to a Life of Courage

The Diving Board

"It's okay, Deb. You can do this!" My husband and my friend coaxed gently, calling across the backyard pool from where they sat on the other side. They knew I was determined to conquer my dread of the diving board and the deep, dark water below. For the moment, I stood with my feet fastened firmly to the safe concrete surface behind the board. Our children splashed and played a few yards away in the shallow end, but they might as well have been a mile from me for the ocean-wide span of deep water that loomed between us. I had resolved that this time would be different. This time, I would finally face my fears, unfasten my feet from the ground where they stubbornly stood, and propel myself forward in an attempt to conquer my fear—my phobia—of the edge of the diving board and what it represented.

My knees knocked and my pulse raced. I tentatively stepped up and onto the platform, then shimmied out until my toes touched the edge. *The edge that dangled over the deepest depths of the pool. The wet, slippery edge that wobbled and wiggled under my timid tootsies as I inched closer toward it.* The voices of my encouragers and the laughter of the children all faded as the blood pounded in my ears. I peered down into the water, and my mind floated back to a long-ago summer in another backyard pool.

Suddenly, I was ten years old again, hearing my name called as I timidly stepped out to the edge of a similar platform. That long-ago summer, families of our rural community had partnered with the YMCA to provide swim lessons for the country kids, using a farm family's pool located a mere fifty miles from town. (Yep, we were really rural.) My parents seized this opportunity, determined that we children would learn to swim. Mom drove us forty miles round trip every day to make it happen. (Did I mention that our farm was even more rural than the pool?) My older sister and I had acquired a few swim basics, and since we were above-average in height and weight for our ages, the instructors took one look at us splashing in shallow water and assumed that our swimming skills were stronger than they really were.

We were placed in the advanced group, where we were expected to swim gracefully across the deep end of the pool like the rest of the class. I tried. But I flapped furiously in an attempt to stay afloat, and that week I found my greatest success in the sinking category. Then came the fateful day when my phobia formed: I had to jump off the diving board.

I nervously stepped up to the platform. The swim instructor coaxed me with reassuring words: "It's okay, Debbie. You can do this. Just step out to the edge. Then jump! I'm right here." She attempted to comfort me, reminding me that she was quite capable of saving me should I need rescue. Eventually, her tone changed, revealing her exasperation. "Debbie, you will jump off this diving board!"

I looked at what appeared to be an impossible situation. Knowing I struggled to stay afloat while merely swimming, I convinced myself that if my chunky frame sank down, it would certainly not be able to bob back up. At all. Ever. But I had no choice. For one thing, there did not appear to be an emergency chute off the side of that platform. (I had checked.) And for another thing, the rear escape route was completely blocked by classmates lined up behind me, actually *excited* for their turn to jump. And for the final thing, there was my frustrated instructor, ordering me from below, where she was treading water. So I slowly stepped out. And then I jumped. Well, sort of. It was more like a clumsy free-fall. And then, forgetting the instructor's reassuring words, I panicked. Down, down, down. My flailing limbs kept me from bobbing back to the surface as I would have done naturally had I simply relaxed. I thought I was a goner. After an eternity, I felt my instructor grab me firmly around the waist and pull me to the surface. She towed me to the side of the pool. While catching her breath after such a feat, she had a few words with me as I sat on the cement, dripping and trembling. "There was nothing to be afraid of, Debbie. If you hadn't panicked, you would have been fine. Why didn't you trust me when I told you I was right here?"

"Don't be afraid, Deb. Just jump off." The calls of my husband and friend jolted me back to the present. And there I was, still standing—me and my timid tootsies—on the edge of the diving board. I had conquered my first fear simply by stepping out *to* the edge. (A major feat for me, considering my phobia.) But if I jumped—if I shot down full-force—would I bob back up? Why couldn't I let go of my fear and step off that wet, slippery edge, letting myself free-fall into the water below? If I panicked, my trusted husband and friend would certainly save me, or at least toss me my froggy floatie or a noodle lifeline and tow me to safety. Why was I so scared? The same fear was paralyzing me from stepping out again, off the edge.

Do Not Be Afraid

I am reminded of the Lord's words to a boatload of fearful disciples: "Do not be afraid." But allow me to back up a bit to the beginning of the story, found in Matthew 14. Mere hours earlier, these men, Jesus' closest followers, had watched Jesus bring divine healing to the masses simply by His touch or a word and out of His great compassion for them. They listened as He proclaimed the kingdom of God to a great crowd and taught them many things. They saw Him give thanks to the Father for a small meal of fish and bread and use it to miraculously feed the thousands who were there. And then they heard Him tell them to step into their boat and go on ahead of Him across the Sea of Galilee, while He dismissed the crowd and retreated to pray.

By evening, a strong wind was raging across the waters, and the disciples were miles from shore, struggling to keep their boat afloat. All night, they battled the wind and the waves. I can only imagine the extent of their fatigue and fear as they fought the dark stormy sea for hours, only to look out on the raging waters at four in the morning and see someone coming toward them, walking on the waves!

We can't know how well the disciples could swim, but we can certainly assume that they were at home on the water. As fishermen, Peter and a handful of Jesus' other disciples spent plenty of time in deep water—at least, in a boat on the deep water. Prior to Jesus' call to follow Him and fish for men, the Sea of Galilee had been a second home to Peter, Andrew, James, and John. And I surmise that on a typical workday, each time these fishermen's tootsies touched the edge of the boat, fear was the furthest thing from their minds as they cast their empty nets and dragged them in, filled with fish.

But in this squall, as the wild sea tossed the little boat, even the bravest fisherman would have quaked with fright to see a figure walking on the choppy waves. No mortal man could do that; the figure had to be something supernatural, right? Matthew 14 tells us they were terrified and cried out in fear, certain they were seeing a ghost. At this, Jesus immediately calmed them with His words: "Take heart; it is I. Do not be afraid" (v. 27). They need not fear, for the One who had so recently healed the crippled, the blind, and the diseased in front of their very eyes was coming to them now. The One who provided sustenance for a hungry multitude was coming to them in the midst of their storm. By walking on the stormy sea, Jesus revealed to them that He is Lord over all creation. They need not be afraid.

When he heard Jesus' reassuring words and saw Him walking toward them, Peter was prompted to step out in faith. Literally. Peter said, "Lord, if it is You, command me to come to You on the water." Jesus said, "Come." So Peter got out of the boat and walked on the water toward Him (vv. 28–29).

I marvel at Peter's impetuous desire to step out of the boat and onto the water so he could be with Jesus. One minute, Peter was terrified, thinking he had seen a ghost; the next minute, he was so excited to see Jesus that he jumped forward in faith onto the stormy sea. As someone who trembles at the mere thought of stepping off a diving board into the calm, clear water of a pool, I cannot imagine saying something akin to "Let me step out into this terrible tempest with You, Jesus!" So before you read the next verses and find fault with Peter's fears, take note of his courage (albeit short-lived) to step out in genuine faith, following Jesus' command to come.

> But when he saw the wind, he was afraid, and beginning to sink he cried out, "Lord, save me." Jesus immediately reached out His hand and took hold of him, saying to him, "O you of little faith, why did you doubt?" (vv. 30–31)

(I warned you about those verses.) What happened to Peter? He stepped out. He was walking *on top of the water* toward Jesus. With eyes focused on the object of his faith, Peter was accomplishing the impossible. "But when he saw the wind, he was afraid." Only when Peter took his eyes off the Lord, looking instead to the apparent impossibility of his situation, did fear overtake him and he began to sink. Peter panicked.

We often picture Peter reaching out his hand, straining to grasp Jesus' extended hand. But we know only that Peter was sinking. I envision him flapping furiously in a futile attempt to stay afloat, as I had all those years ago during swimming lessons. Jesus immediately took hold of His floundering follower. Perhaps He grabbed hold of Peter's arm, his hand, or even his waist, much as my swim instructor had grabbed hold of me. In the same way she reached out to me and then gently scolded me for my lack of trust, so did the Savior grab hold of Peter and tenderly rebuke him for his faltering faith. In the midst of Peter's fear and doubt, Jesus saved him.

What about you and me?

The scary place we're in may look different from a stormy sea or a backyard diving board, but the effect is much the same: fear paralyzes us. Or perhaps, like Peter, we have taken some first steps forward in faith while focused on our Savior, obediently following Him and trusting Him to accomplish His work through us. And then, *whammo!* The wind and waves of this world grab our attention, and our gaze shifts to them. They look so big and menacing; they distract us and threaten to overtake us.

In our fear, our eyes move away from Him to our often-scary circumstances: the daunting task that lies before us; the intimidating employer who placed our job on the chopping block; the frightening medical prognosis for us or for a loved one. Maybe we are afraid to try something new because we may get hurt. Perhaps it's our pride that will suffer if we are mocked, ridiculed, or criticized for sharing our faith and moral convictions. We stare wild-eyed into our fear of failure, of rejection, of the unknown. Our focus is diverted from our Savior to the uncertainty, difficulty, or apparent impossibility of our situations. Flapping furiously, we find ourselves sinking further beneath our tsunami-size fear. Paralyzed in our panic, we cannot come up for air, let alone move forward on our own. Like Peter, we cry out, "Lord, save me," and already He is there, for He knows our need.

Jesus Steps In

The Lord reaches out and grabs hold of us in the midst of our sin and fear. Saving. Guiding. Replacing our fear with faith as He tows us to His side. In His Word, He gently rebukes us for our lack of trust, reminding us that He is always with us and is completely capable of saving us. Strengthened by faith in Jesus, we are able to turn our gaze back to Him. Safe in the His grip, we can step out of our fears, no matter how big or menacing they seem, trusting that He is even bigger! We need not be afraid.

Because Jesus steps in, we can step out. By the Spirit's leading, we can step out of the fears that threaten to distract us, pull us under, and paralyze us. We can step out in faith and obedience to follow Him and do what He calls us to do, confident that He holds us, protects us, and guides us each step of the way. The Holy Spirit fills us with courage to step out with trust that Jesus can and will accomplish the impossible through us. In Christ, we can undertake that daunting task with confidence; we can handle possible ridicule or rejection with grace as we share our faith; we can face the unknown with the calm assurance that we will never walk alone.

> And when they got into the boat, the wind
> ceased. And those in the boat worshiped Him,
> saying, "Truly You are the Son of God." (vv. 32–33)

Remember that Jesus grabbed hold of Peter while the storm continued to rage. Only after He brought His frightened disciple safely to the boat did Jesus calm the storm. Why? Perhaps to show all of His followers that He can be trusted in the calm and in the storm. Or perhaps to show us that while He might not choose to save us from a storm, He holds us close and protects us while the storm rages about us. Our scary circumstances may not change, but by His grace, *we* do. We grow in trust as He carries us through the storms of life and brings our focus back to Him. And our response, prompted by the Holy Spirit, is that of His first followers. In awe of His saving love for us, we are compelled to worship Him, the Son of God, our Savior!

Focus: The Three Os

Even when our focus has been disrupted by the troubles of the world or by the lies of Satan, the fact remains that our very identity, purpose, and protection are all found in Christ. Nothing in this world and no lies of the evil one can alter these facts. Satan can only attempt to divert our focus. While our physical eyes may be distracted by the crashing waves, by God's grace, our spiritual eyes are opened to see that He is right there in the waves, larger than this life and capable of quieting our fears, quieting the storm, or both!

Isn't it comforting to know that God knows and understands that you will face fear in this world of sin and struggles? As He enables you to fix your eyes on Him, you can focus on His **omniscience**—His knowledge of all things—and you can admit any and all fears to Him. "I sought the LORD, and He answered me and delivered me from all my fears" (Psalm 34:4). Cry out to Jesus and confess your fears to Him. His Word concerning those fears speaks directly to your heart to let you know that He will deliver you from them. Throughout the Scriptures, our all-knowing God comforts His people, telling them not to be afraid as they face their enemies, as they enter uncharted territory, as they walk in obedience to His commands. As He reaches out to you again and again, He leads you to put your trust in Him with each new fear and every situation; He tells you, "Do not be afraid." And like the psalmist, we can say, "When I am afraid, I put my trust in You" (Psalm 56:3).

As the Lord fills you with trust in Him, focus on His **omnipotence,** His all-powerful ability to overcome all things—even sin, death, and the devil—by His death and resurrection. Again, fear subsides. Jesus said, "In the world you will have tribulation. But take heart; I have overcome the world" (John 16:33). Maybe your tribulation—your scary situation—will improve, but even if it doesn't, you can trust that your Savior is changing *you* as He divinely intervenes, working on your behalf, producing in you greater trust, and working all things together for good for you who are called according to His purpose (Romans 8:28).

Focus on His **omnipresence.** He is with you always; you are not alone! "It is the LORD who goes before you. He will be with you; He will not leave you or forsake you. Do not fear or be dismayed" (Deuteronomy 31:8). The One who knit you together in your mother's womb is with you now. The One who redeemed you from your sin and filled you with faith by the power of the Holy Spirit comes to you in the midst of your storms. The One who is able to shelter you with His powerful protection also quiets you with His continuous presence. There is no place you can go apart from His presence (Psalm 139:7–10). He goes before you, walks beside you, and holds you by His right hand. You need not be afraid.

A Stepping-Out Story

From the time he was a toddler and throughout his elementary years, Kyle was always a happy-go-lucky kid. Grinning from ear to ear, he often had a joke to tell or some silly humor to share. His parents, Kip and Deb, and his little sister, Katie, were entertained for hours by Kyle's antics. His pastors and Sunday School teachers always knew they were in for a treat when Kyle entered the room. He was an outspoken child, full of questions and eager to talk about his faith and happy to throw in a few sports statistics here and there for good measure.

When Kyle was twelve, during the middle of his fall soccer season, he began experiencing pain in his left leg, even though he had not sustained any kind of injury. Before long, he was walking with a noticeable limp. Kip and Deb took him to have it examined. Kip called our house with the dev-

astating news that their greatest fear had been realized—
Kyle had been diagnosed with osteosarcoma, bone cancer
found in his femur.

Deb told me, "It was as if we were punched in the stomach when we first received the news." She and her husband
are physicians. They know all too well the potential outcomes from this type of cancer. Had they focused only on
their very scary situation, fear could have engulfed them.
At first, Deb distracted herself with busyness, focusing on
each day's tasks for Kyle, doing everything she *could* do so
she wouldn't think too much about all that she could *not* do
for him, all of those terrifying things that were out of her
control.

Right there, in the midst of her fear, God filled Deb with
trust. She and her husband believe that their Savior is so
much bigger than the manifestation of their greatest fear.
"We trusted that God wanted the best for Kyle," Deb said.
"The Lord loves him even more than we do." She knew their
faith had to outweigh their fear. "If we gave into fear, we
wouldn't have been any good to anybody, especially Kyle."
Over and over, they laid their fears before the Lord. "God,
You're in control. We look to You. According to Your will
and Your timing, please bring healing to our son. Increase
our faith; grant us strength and courage."

Kyle's parents did everything they could for him, all the
while clinging to the Lord for strength; and as they did, God
continually showed them how He was working mightily in
and through their child. From the beginning of the battle,
Kyle was able to keep his eyes on the Lord and maintain a

positive outlook toward his treatments. Kyle reported, "The doctors let me push the start button on my IV pump, so *I* officially started my own chemo."

Soon after he was diagnosed, Kyle recognized that his fellow seventh-grade students had their own fears. So he stepped in front of the class and spoke encouragingly before them. He reassured them that he stood a good chance of beating the cancer, even if that meant the amputation of his leg. And if that were to happen, he said would plan to become a motivational speaker and share his story to bring cheer to other kids with cancer. With a twinkle in his eyes, he told them that if he didn't beat it, he would get to be with Jesus even sooner! Kyle says confidently that he knows one day he will go to heaven, no matter the outcome of his cancer.

Always a huge Nebraska Huskers fan, and quite a humorist, Kyle chose to bring a smile to his loved ones following his first treatment. After nausea hit him, he admitted on his CaringBridge site that his sickness could have been due to the chemo, but could also have been a reaction to the Huskers' game performance (or lack thereof) that day! He loved to say that his Huskers couldn't be beat. Kyle's classmates and friends responded, "Kyle, *you* can't be beat!"

Treatments followed treatments, then major surgery, and still more treatments. Mouth sores and nausea, hair loss and missed school, crutches and therapy were just some of the many difficulties Kyle had to contend with in the year that followed. With all of this behind them now, Kyle and his family look ahead, hopeful that he will continue to receive a positive prognosis and focused on their Savior for continued strength. Their faith in Christ and the witness they have shared throughout this time have touched countless lives, from hospital staff to sports celebrities, from close friends to complete strangers. The Lord has enabled many people to see how He has used this scary trial for His good.

Looking back, Deb shares, "During this ordeal, I was reminded that God gives us our kids for such a short time. Kyle is mine, but he really isn't; he belongs to the Lord. And our lives here are so short compared to eternity. Our trial was made easier when we compared it to an eternity with Jesus free of fear, trials, and pain."

Every class in Kyle's Lutheran school posted prayers for him during his early treatments. The words of faith that flowed from these children expressed their honesty as they, too, faced fear on behalf of their friend. "Give Kyle and his family the strength to overcome this scary ordeal" (eighth grader). "Kyle needs Your help. Please keep him in Your hands, Lord" (third grader). "Lord, when he is nervous and scared, let him remember to turn to You. Even through his illness, You are allowing him to share his faith with others" (fifth grader).

The simple prayer that follows was written by a class of precious preschoolers whose childlike faith is shown in their words. Their prayer can remind us to keep our eyes focused on our Great Provider as we bring all our concerns to Him: "God, we thought of things Kyle may need to get better. Things like hugs and kisses, medicine, jelly beans, a soft bed, books, prune juice, a pillow pet, dollies, music, a good doctor, a cold rag, and milk with cookies. We know You will give him all he needs, because You love him so much."

Yes, God loves Kyle so much. He loves you that much too. God will give you all you need. He will trade your doubts for faith, exchange your weakness for His strength, and replace your fears with rock-solid courage found only in Him. If you face life-threatening trials and scary situations, He is able to fill you with peace, patience, and a positive outlook, as only He can. "And my God will supply every need of yours according to His riches in glory in Christ Jesus" (Philippians 4:19).

Life on the Edge

Maybe you are wondering, "Did she do it? Did she conquer her fear of the diving board? Was she able to step off the edge and free-fall into the deep end?" My answer is a resounding, "Not yet." (That's not much of a resounding answer, is it?) But I haven't given up trying. Perhaps one day I will finally conquer that phobia. In the meantime, the Lord has enabled me to find through it a powerful paradigm that I share with you in this chapter. I may struggle to jump off the edge of a diving board, but I have conquered my first fear by stepping *to* the edge, time and time again. You see, moving from the safe place behind the board, stepping onto the platform, and then shimmying all the way out to the wet, slippery edge symbolizes "stepping out" of so much more, as we will explore in the following chapters.

I can step out of my fears only because I am backed by the power of Christ to go to a place where He would have me live courageously, a place where I am no longer paralyzed by fear or sinking in it but where I am living boldly for Him in every part of my life. My Savior beckons, "Follow Me," as He extends His hand to lead me to a place where I dare not tread alone. And if I should ever shrink back in fear, retreating to the back of the board, He will lovingly draw me to the edge once again.

Jesus gives me courage to live my life of service for Him. He moves me to a life on the edge, where I can live fearlessly and securely in God's will, centered on the solid foundation of Christ.

What might this edgy living look like?

• Taking a healthy risk to try something new or taking on that daunting task with courage.

• Standing up for my faith in the face of criticism or danger.

• Trusting His will for my life, in the midst of scary circumstances and down the unknown path that lies ahead.

Reflections

1. Look back to former fears and scary situations. How did things turn out? How did God protect you or others, and how did He use that situation to grow your trust in Him?

2. Read Matthew 14:22–33. As you do, place your feet in Peter's soggy sandals. Imagine his range of emotions as he witnessed Christ's miracles on land and later on the sea. Next, imagine stepping out of the boat to meet the Lord on the water, only to freeze in fear, and finally to feel His firm grip as He saves.

3. Is a traumatic memory haunting you, causing you to continually live in fear? Explain.

4. Is something in your present world causing you to tremble with fear? What may be stopping you in your tracks, halting you from stepping out? Ask God to help you identify your present fears. Pray that He would help you lift your eyes up and away from the focus of your fears and into the face of Jesus, the object of your faith. Ask for His strength to overcome those fears so that you may be able to step out in faith.

5. Read Psalm 139:7–10. How do the psalmist's words bring you comfort and courage as you focus on the Lord's omnipresence?

6. How might the Lord be working on your behalf, in the midst of your scary situation? Let these promises from His Word speak to you, concerning your fear:
Psalm 27:1; Psalm 56:11; John 14:27; Hebrews 13:6

7. What might your life on the edge look like as you step out of your fear, by the Spirit's power, into a courageous place where Christ would have you live?

Write further
reflections here

CHAPTER TWO

Stepping Out of

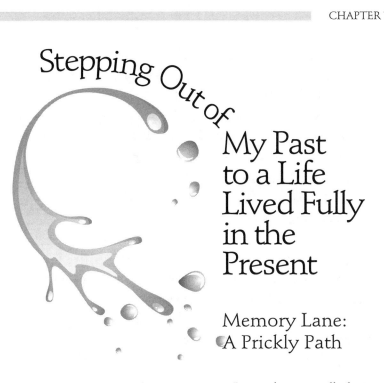

My Past to a Life Lived Fully in the Present

Memory Lane: A Prickly Path

I am taking a walk down memory lane again, only this time it's more of a prickly path. Instead of gazing back on a trail of fun adventures and favorite memories (and there are plenty of them), I am stuck—again—in a stinky place, rehashing my major regrets and mess-ups, my foibles and failures.

This time, my mind has wandered to a tense conversation with a friend several years ago. I had just found out that she and her husband had given up on their marriage; they were getting a divorce. I didn't see it coming, and I was angry. Angry with her for failing to try any longer. Angry that they had not sought counseling. Angry that I had to find out about it from someone else. So when she came to me that morning, seeking a friend who would listen, what she received instead was some untimely counsel and a lot of "Yes, buts . . ." I wanted desperately for her to see her husband's point of view, but in the process, I failed to see hers. Not only were my words poorly chosen, but I also turned the deaf ear to the pain she was trying to express to me.

I have wondered many times, *If I had handled our conversation differently, might the outcome have been different?* Maybe she would have given her marriage another try. I could have been there for her, but in my anger, I chose not to be. For months, even as my family sought to help hers, she and I communicated very little. I live with the regret of what might have been following that pivotal conversation and the lack of positive interaction in the months thereafter. Although we eventually reconnected and talked through some of the pain, we never communicated again with the level of trust and transparency that we had once shared. My words changed our friendship. Yes, this is a segment of the prickly path from my past that I plod down again and again.

Another regret is the time I failed to take action. Right after we married, my husband and I rented a townhouse. Although we knew it was located in a rough neighborhood, the price was right and our time there would be brief. The walls were thin; we heard more than we cared to from the neighbors next door. I will never forget hearing the cries of a child as his stepfather physically abused him. I knew I should confront the man or report to the authorities what I had heard, but I was too scared. *What would the man do to me? Would I have to appear in court?* So I remained silent. Looking back now, I question myself over and over why

I didn't at least file a report. At the time, I did not want to get involved; I did not even want to think about the cries that I heard. For years, I have wondered what happened to the child. Could I have made a difference by taking action? This, too, is a segment of the worn-out path I continue to tread upon.

I pound the ground on those same old trails and others. I regret decisions I made during college. I bemoan the times I failed to share my Christian witness with an acquaintance. I rehash hurtful conversations or interactions with family and friends—everything from opposing political viewpoints to differing perspectives on the rearing of children. (Good grief!) Along the way, because of my actions, communication has often been stifled and relationships have suffered.

Some of my rehashed regrets were downright silly; others were very serious. But all have threatened to stop me in my tracks and prevent me from moving forward in regard to making good decisions, sharing my faith, and enjoying rich relationships with open and honest communication.

Are your failures and regrets from the past threatening to prevent you from living life fully in the present? Do you find yourself stuck on the same well-beaten path, continuing to tread over the same trampled ground? Maybe you are still stewing over yesterday (or twenty years ago), berating yourself with thoughts such as "I should have talked to her"; "I should never have done that dreadful thing to him"; or "If they knew what I did way back then, they wouldn't want to be friends with me now." Satan loves to have us dwell on hurtful past events such as that awful argument we had with our mother, that terrible thing we did to our friend, or that lie we told that ruined a relationship.

The enemy would have us constantly looking back over our shoulder, peering into the past, focusing on our former sins, failures, and regrets. He may even whisper such lies as "You will never get over this. You will always struggle with that past sin holding you captive. Just give up. After all you have done, God could never forgive you, and neither could anyone else."

You know what happens if you don't look where you're going—you trip. It is difficult to take even one step forward when we are so busy looking back, stumbling backward down those same old trails. We struggle so much to live in the present that we can't look to the future.

As we despair over the past, we may think that the sins of yesterday disqualify us from any happiness today, that our former failures exclude us from the Body of Christ in His Church, and that our mess-ups of the past prohibit us from living a respectable life in the present and in the future. We listen to these lies and allow them to condemn us.

Then Jesus steps in!

His Word promises us, "There is therefore now no condemnation for those who are in Christ Jesus. For the law of the Spirit of life has set you free in Christ Jesus from the law of sin and death" (Romans 8:1–2).

We don't have to fall for the enemy's lies! We are no longer condemned for our sins, because we are forgiven in Christ. Led by the Holy Spirit, we can look to the Lord with a repentant heart. As Jesus grabs hold of us, He leads us to step out of the past, sorry for our sins and trusting in His forgiveness and grace to cleanse us completely: "If we confess our sins, He is faithful and just to forgive us our sins and to cleanse us from all unrighteousness" (1 John 1:9).

Just as Jesus steps into our lives and enables us to step out of the past, so He stepped into the life of a woman in Samaria, as recorded in the Gospel of John.

Forgiven and Free!

In John 4, we read that Jesus and His disciples were traveling from Judea to Galilee, taking a direct route through Samaria. Most Jews would have used a different route to avoid Samaria and its inhabitants, whom they had despised for centuries. But it was necessary that Jesus journey this way on that day, because it was God's plan that a divine encounter take place there.

Jesus was weary from the journey, and at noon of the day, He stopped by Jacob's well outside the Samaritan city of Sychar. It was customary for the women of the area to meet at the well in the evening to draw water for their families' needs; they likely assisted one another and interacted in friendly fashion as they ended their day's work. But this was noon. Jesus' disciples had gone into town to buy lunch. He was likely alone as He sat down to rest, as few people would have come to the well in the heat of the day.

As Jesus sat there under the noonday sun, a Samaritan woman came to draw water. We learn in later verses that she was of moral question. The townspeople would have known of her past, would have known the life she currently lived. She was probably not welcome in their midst and most likely would not have been invited to join the rest of the women at the customary water-drawing hour. So this was probably just another ordinary day for the unnamed Samaritan woman who came alone to draw water. Another ordinary day, that is, until Jesus stepped into her life.

When the woman approached the well, Jesus tested her, asking her to give Him a drink. Because Jews did not associate with the despised Samaritans, the woman was shocked that this Jewish man would even speak to her, let alone ask her to do something for Him! But we know that there was a special purpose to Jesus' testing of this woman so stained with sin. Jesus told her if she only knew who it was asking her for a drink, that *she* would be asking *Him!* And He would give her "living water"—the gift of God!

"Jesus said to her, 'Everyone who drinks of this water will be thirsty again, but whoever drinks of the water that I will give him will never be thirsty again. The water that I will give him will become in him a spring of water welling up to eternal life'" (John 4:13–14). Jesus stepped into her world, reached out with His grace, and offered her living water—salvation in His name, eternal life!

Jesus went on to test her further, revealing that He knew everything about her sordid, sinful past. "Jesus said to her, 'Go, call your husband, and come here.' The woman answered Him, 'I have no husband.' Jesus said to her, 'You are right in saying, "I have no husband"; for you have had five husbands, and the one you now have is not your husband. What you have said is true'" (vv. 16–18). Jesus then revealed to her that He was the promised Messiah—the Christ. Imagine how her heart must have leaped at this news; how dramatically her life changed in just a few moments. The man who stood before her was the promised one, the Messiah Himself! He knew all about her past and her shame, her mistakes and her willfully unscrupulous decisions. He knew everything she had ever done, and still He came to her and extended His forgiving love, offering her His promise of salvation, the gift of eternal life.

What was her response? She was so excited, John tells us, that she left her water jar at the well and made tracks for town. She ran to the townspeople—people who would have shunned her—and told them, "Come, see a man who told me all that I ever did. Can this be the Christ?" (v. 29)"

Because Jesus stepped in, the Samaritan woman could step out in faith and confidence. She could not keep this Good News to herself. She couldn't help but shout it to her world! John tells us that because of her testimony, many people believed in Jesus that day. Through one forgiven woman, the Lord brought many to receive His free gift of faith. Although we don't know what became of the Samaritan woman, we trust that her life was never the same. Gone was the sin of the past that once held her captive. Forgiven and free, she received the refreshing water of grace that comes only through Christ!

This is God's grace; this is the unmerited favor He has for you, just as He had for the Samaritan woman. No great big ugly sin you have committed is a match for the size of His grace given to you. In His rich and generous forgiveness and mercy, you are set free. Free from the grip of sin and the sting of death. God gives you victory over all the sins of your past that once held you captive, all because of His great love for you in His Son, Jesus Christ, who paid the price for all the world's sin through His death on the cross.

God knows where you have been and what you have done. Lost or broken, addicted or ashamed; still stumbling down a trail full of former failures or regrets. You are found by Him; you are forgiven and free, restored and renewed, made whole and holy in His name.

"Therefore, if anyone is in Christ, he is a new creation. The old has passed away; behold, the new has come (2 Corinthians 5:17). You are a new creation! The old you— the sinner of the past—is gone; the new you—a new creation in Christ—has come. Ask the Lord to help you move past the past. To step out of the past so you may live fully in the present. He has already forgiven you. And He can help you forgive yourself.

A Stepping-Out Story

Hers was the first friendly face that I recall seeing during our early-Sunday-morning visit to the church that we would soon call home. Melanie greeted me warmly and with genuine interest asked questions about my family. She was sincere in her offer to help us get acclimated to the city and to the church. Before long, she was calling to ask if I would like to join her for a women's small-group Bible study.

As I got to know Melanie, I learned that our children were the same age and that we were both stay-at-home moms.

We shared bubbly personalities, and we both liked to talk—a lot. I liked this woman from the start! And there was something intriguing about Melanie that I admired. She was comfortable in her own skin, content with who she was. I was delighted to be near her, because her caring personality and easy laughter made me feel accepted and free to be myself too. Melanie spoke so knowledgeably about the Scriptures that I assumed she was a lifelong student of the Word. She shared openly about God's grace in Christ, the certainty of forgiveness that we have in His name, and the confidence in our salvation that we receive by faith in our Savior. Melanie taught me much about grace by the way she lived her life.

Our weekly Bible study became a trusted place of sharing joys and struggles, frustrations and fears, and even past sins and regrets. And that is where Melanie spoke candidly. Much to my amazement, she was not a lifelong Christian. In her childhood home, higher education was valued, but faith in a higher being was not. In fact, religion was not discussed at all. Because her parents were nonbelievers and looked to science to answer all of life's questions, it was easy for Melanie to come to her own conclusion that there was no God. She was a self-proclaimed atheist.

Determined to live her life as she saw fit, Melanie completed her higher education and began a career. Meanwhile, she was enjoying life in the fast lane, partying as she pleased, making one unscrupulous decision after another. For her at that time, life was all about having fun, so the minute something or someone stopped being fun, she moved on to something else. If a relationship went south, she believed it was time to get out. Melanie endured two failed marriages and a handful of other relationships before meeting and marrying her third husband, with whom she began to raise a family.

Melanie still gave no thought to God, until her firstborn turned two and she began to consider her child's future education. Because this was a high priority for her, Melanie and her husband explored the local educational options and learned about the Lutheran school down the road. Melanie called to inquire about the school, and the pastor said simply, "You should come to church Sunday." Completely oblivious as to what this might mean, she told her husband, "We need to find out more about the school, so we have to visit the church."

Melanie recalls with great detail the flippant attitude she had as she seated herself in the pew that first Sunday morning. She heard God's Word read and proclaimed, but she refused to bow her head or even pretend to pray. She didn't sing a word of a hymn but sat stiffly through the service. She said with a smirk that lightning from heaven would surely strike her, right there in the middle of the worship service, because she was "playing pretend" as she sat in the house of the Lord with His faithful followers. Despite her attitude, when the pastor met Melanie and her family after church and asked if he could visit that very afternoon, she agreed.

Although she did not recognize it that day, God was at work on her heart, and Melanie returned to church week after week. When the pastor invited her to the adult instruction class, again she was oblivious, thinking, *What can this hurt? It's education. I have always liked being in class . . .* Several sessions later, as the pastor talked about faith and Baptism, he rocked her world with these simple words, "Melanie, it is clear that you have faith."

How could that be? She knew she wanted no part of this Christian faith, and yet there it was! The Holy Spirit had been working through God's Word over the past months, instilling faith in Melanie's heart, even though she hadn't been seeking it. "I came kicking and screaming into the faith!" Melanie laughs with joy now as she tells the story again. The Lord chose Melanie, calling her out of the darkness of death and disbelief and into His marvelous light by His grace. She found out that her husband had been praying for her—and this was God's glorious answer!

In the weeks and months that followed, she learned so much more about this faith that she now possessed by the grace of God. In a Sunday morning Bible class full of scholars and professors, Melanie courageously asked question after question. "When you are the new student, as I was, it's clear that you don't know anything, so it's easy to put yourself out there and ask. And no one had a problem telling me when I was wrong," she recalls with a chuckle.

But the shadow of her past still loomed over her. Despite the fact that she was a believer, chosen by the Lord and growing in His Word, she wondered how He could forgive her for the sins of her past; her guilt had been bottled up for so long. "When you're not a Christian, you have to deal with the guilt of sin somehow. You can say it's not a sin because you don't recognize that there is such a thing. And you aren't sorry to God because you don't have a god. You can find people who are worse sinners than you. You can hide within the law of the land, telling yourself that what's legal must be okay. You can justify sin all you like. But you cannot get rid of it. The guilt is still a burden. You may not recognize it at the time, but it's still there."

Before long, Melanie joined a small-group Bible study for moms (the very group I would join years later). When she summoned the courage to share her stormy past with the women in the group, she admits, "What I expected was condemnation, but what I got was grace." She thought, *If these human Christians can show me this kind of grace, then maybe God can forgive me too.* The women encouraged Melanie to talk to the pastor about her past. She did, and he assured her of God's complete forgiveness in Christ. "All have sinned and fall short of the glory of God, and are justified by His grace as a gift, through the redemption that is in Christ Jesus" (Romans 3:23–24).

With His mighty power, Jesus stepped into Melanie's life, grabbed hold of her, and walked with her, enabling her to step out of the past and into a joy-filled life of freedom and forgiveness—a life on the edge. This was the confident-in-Christ woman whom I met and liked from the start! Today, Melanie can speak so candidly about her past because she is no longer held captive by it. The guilt she could not get rid of on her own is gone. "There is only One who can take it away, and that's God," she says. "And He did. I am free!"

Melanie says she is comfortable with confessing her past publicly because it puts a familiar face on sin. Too often, it is easy to convict people we don't know, to sit in the judgment seat over them. It is much harder to look at another Christian with condemnation when she says to you, "I've committed that sin, and God has forgiven me." She humbly hopes God will use her to open others' eyes to see His amazing grace and how they can extend that grace to others.

Life on the Edge

Here are a few pivotal points I have learned on my walk to the scary end of the diving board, as Jesus enables me to step out of my past to a life on the edge:

- I don't deserve His forgiveness for that great big ugly sin. None of us does. The fact is, we are not deserving of a second chance, or a third, or a one-hundred-and-third. And by the way, we may categorize and weigh sin differently, from "great big ugly" to "little white lie," but all sin is equally offensive to God, and it all separates us from Him. We are all in need of a Savior from our sin. And that's the beauty of grace: freely receiving what we don't deserve. Pardon. Mercy. Unmerited favor.

- My former failures do not dictate who I am today. The sins of my past do not have to continue to *de*fine me, but God can use those rough spots to *re*fine me as He shapes me continually into His Son's image. His saving love for us and His continual work in us define us and make us who we are: forgiven children of God in Christ. In Christ—wow! Our identity is found in *Him*, not in our past. Not in what we've done or failed to do, where we've been, or what the world says about us based on our past. Knowing my identity is in Christ, I can step out into the world, confident that He will use my life witness to reach others for Him.

- I am not to remember my past sins to the extent that I am weighed down by them or stuck in them. You and I are forgiven and free. Therefore, there is only one healthy reason the Lord may have us remember the regrets of yesterday: to learn from them as He molds us into the image of His Son, our Savior. We may also use the memory or experience of our sin to step out and approach the people affected by those past mistakes so we may seek their forgiveness too.

How do we move ahead, stepping out of the past to a life on the edge? We do it by facing forward. We peer straight into the face of Jesus, and by His amazing grace, we take that first baby step. Perhaps some days it will feel more like plodding, placing one foot laboriously in front of the other. No matter; each step is by His strength alone, walking in the Word and trusting in His promises, regardless of how we feel. And when we fall backward, He is there to catch us, enabling us to get back up and plod forward again. We rest in the truth that His mercies are never-ending; they are brand new every day: "The steadfast love of the LORD never ceases; His mercies never come to an end; they are new every morning" (Lamentations 3:22–23).

Reflections

1. Do your failures and regrets from the past threaten to prevent you from living life fully in the present? Do you find yourself stuck on the same well-beaten, prickly path, continuing to trod over the same trampled ground? Explain.

2. Read John 4:3–30, 39–42. As you do, place yourself in the Samaritan woman's sandals during her initial encounter with Jesus, as He extends to her the gift of eternal life, when He reveals to her that He is the Messiah, and as she tells the townspeople the greatest of news! Share your thoughts and insights.

3. The apostle Paul spoke candidly about his past as a Pharisee. So zealous for the Law was he that he used his authority to persecute, imprison, and oversee the stoning of early Christians. (See Acts 22:4; 26:9–10 for some of Paul's words concerning his former way of life.)

Then God called Paul out of the darkness and into the light of His grace. Read about God's grace in Paul's life—past, present, and future—in 1 Corinthians 15:9–10a and Philippians 3:13b–14.

4. Reflect on and respond to this statement: "The sins of my past do not have to continue to *define* me, but God can use those rough spots to *refine* me as He shapes me continually into His Son's image."

5. Read aloud: "Therefore, if anyone is in Christ, he is a new creation. The old has passed away; behold, the new has come" (2 Corinthians 5:17). Say a prayer of praise and thanksgiving that God has made you brand-new in Christ. The old is gone; the new has come. You are forgiven and free.

6. How might the Lord use something from your past to enable you to minister to someone today?

7. What might your life on the edge look like, as you step out of your past by the Spirit's power and fully into the present, where Christ would have you live?

Write further
reflections here

CHAPTER THREE

Stepping Out of My Worries to a Life of Trust

Worrywart

That's me. A worrywart. I could give you a running list of all the "worries of the day," kind of like the daily specials at your local restaurant. There is always something new and different to add to the menu, along with the returning favorites over which I continually stew (yes, stew is certainly on the menu!). Whether the *du jour* menu items have to do with relationships or finances, safety or provision, all contain the same main ingredient: worry.

Even as a child, I found countless things to worry about. One time, when I was in fourth grade, a classmate informed me that her parents were divorcing, and then she defensively announced that mine could be next. Although I had no rational reason to believe her words that were blurted out in anger and pain, I began to worry: *What if . . . ?* Another time, when my older sister, Connie, started to drive, I worried we would have a wreck on our way home from our little rural school. One day, I was so certain of it that I forced her to stop the car so I could get out and walk the gravel roads all the way home, sparing myself from certain catastrophe. Of course, Connie arrived home safely long before I did, and she was much less exhausted.

Then there was the worry over my younger sister. Not an average little girl, Lisa was born with a rare degenerative form of epilepsy. She was a hyperactive child who feared nothing, in sharp contrast to me, who worried about everything, especially her. While my family had legitimate reason for concern over her safety and health, I often managed to take that concern to the next level: an unhealthy degree of anxiety and worry. One memory, in particular, stands out.

Fearless Little Shepherd

When the sheep rancher down the road found himself with eighteen motherless lambs in need of care, my father allowed my sisters and me to adopt these little critters and spend the summer caring for them. Unique markings on each lamb made it easy to distinguish one from another, and Connie decided they each needed a name. We spent countless hours in the sheep pen each day, bottle-feeding and petting, playing and lying down beside our little flock.

Lisa had a way with the sheep; she was a true shepherd. When she called them, they listened. On several occasions, the lambs found a hole in the fence and followed one another out of the pen to wander away. Lisa found them, bawling and bleating. She called the sheep by name, clucked her tongue, and walked ahead of them. Every lamb followed her in faithful procession. Sometimes, she would scoop up one of the lambs into her small arms and carry it here and there. Oblivious to the potential threat of rattlesnakes and other dangerous creatures that occasionally roamed our prairie ranch, Lisa would often lie down in the tall grass in or out of the pen, surrounded by her flock. My parents and Connie and I all marveled at our fearless little shepherd.

But I was carried away by my anxiety. In my vivid imagination, I often envisioned rattlesnakes attacking Lisa or the sheep. I worried she wouldn't be able to tell us if she had been bitten. I feared we would find her lying unconscious in the pen. While I breathed a sigh of relief every time she stepped in the house, I secretly inspected her arms and legs to make sure there were no telltale bites (as if they wouldn't have been obvious!). I was too embarrassed by my irrational worries to let anyone else know. That is what a worrywart does.

Meanwhile, in Lisa's little world, there was no room for worry. She cared for the sheep and led them to safety. Because of her love for the sheep, our fearless little shepherd would have placed herself between a snake and her flock, if necessary. That is what a shepherd does.

I learned a lot from my worry-free little shepherd, and yet today I still fall into the same anxiety traps in my daily walk, making mountains out of molehills. I fuss about the future with thoughts such as, "What is this world coming to?" I worry that my teenage children will get in some kind of accident as I fret over their safety: "Honey, don't chew gum while walking. What if you trip? You'll choke!" I agonize over commitments and deadlines: "I won't be able to successfully complete what I have started. I'll fail and disappoint everyone, including myself." (My kids call that "epic fail.") I fret about finances. I stress over relationships. I stew over perfect strangers' opinions of me. I worry that I or a loved one will wind up with cancer. Far too often, I ask, "What if . . . ," and then I stew over the possible outcomes should my what-if worries become realities.

My mind wanders into a wilderness of worry, consuming much of my energy and getting me nowhere. *Whew!* Worry wears me out!

Of course, there are such things as legitimate care and concern. Some matters deserve our attention and action. (We train our children to look both ways before crossing the street. We learn the importance of financial stewardship. We visit the doctor for regular checkups. We give attention to our relationships.) And a certain level of anxiety can be healthy too; it can drive us to meet deadlines and complete those tasks that deserve our time and attention. But other matters are beyond our control or fall into the category of irrational "what ifs." So why do we foolishly stray into those unhealthy places of worry again and again?

Comfort in Christ, the Good Shepherd

How often do we, like my sister's foster sheep, wander away from Christ's trustworthy care and wind up in an anxious, troubled place? What hole in the fence of faith have we found to crawl through? What worries lead us to stray from our confidence in Him?

The answers are as unique as we are. But no matter how far we wander in our sin, our Good Shepherd seeks us and calls us by name; He steps in, calms our anxious hearts, and leads us to a safe place of trust. In our Baptism, the Lord marked us as His own and imparted His Holy Spirit just for us. The Spirit fills us with faith in our Savior, the great Shepherd of His sheep, who laid down His life for us. That is what the Good Shepherd does.

We can find comfort and courage in these words of Christ:

> The sheep hear his voice, and he calls his own sheep by name and leads them out. When he has brought out all his own, he goes before them, and the sheep follow him, for they know his voice. . . . I am the good shepherd. The good shepherd lays down his life for the sheep. . . . I am the good shepherd. I know My own and My own know Me, just as the Father knows Me and I know the Father; and I lay down My life for the sheep. (John 10:3–4, 11, 14–15)

By the power of His Spirit, we know our Savior's voice, and we listen to Him as He speaks to us in His Word and as He calls us by name, leading us and guiding us into His truth. He goes before us, and we follow because we trust Him. We need not worry senselessly about anything, for our Good Shepherd, who willingly laid down His life for us, now scoops us up in His strong arms and carries us.

He holds fast to you; you are and will remain firmly in His grip. In Luke 12:22–34, Jesus tenderly told His disciples not to be anxious or to worry about their lives. He said,

"Fear, not, little flock, for it is your Father's good pleasure to give you the kingdom" (v. 32). Your Creator recognizes and knows your needs and concerns even better than you do. You are a precious little lamb in the Savior's flock. He has chosen to give you abundant and eternal life, here and in heaven.

Jesus Steps In

What worries make you wander? Whatever they are, you can take heart. Look to His promises regarding His continual protection and provision, His presence and His peace. Jesus said, "Peace I leave with you; My peace I give to you. Not as the world gives do I give to you. Let not your hearts be troubled, neither let them be afraid" (John 14:27). Trust the Lord, by the power of the Spirit, to lovingly lead you through each worry even when, by human reason and understanding, you can see no way past it. Because He steps in, you can trust and step out. Know that He "is able to do far more abundantly than all that we ask or think, according to the power at work within us" (Ephesians 3:20). He is your strength; He enables you to step out of worry!

Jesus stepped into the lives of all the people who followed Him in countless crowds wherever He went. On one such occasion, He climbed up the side of a mountain and gave what we know as the Sermon on the Mount, as recorded in Matthew 5–7. A sizable section in chapter 6 is devoted to worry. Imagine that! Then, as now, people were often consumed with worry and anxiety. Let's check out His words:

Therefore I tell you, do not be anxious about your
life, what you will eat or what you will drink, nor
about your body, what you will put on. Is not life
more than food, and the body more than clothing?
Look at the birds of the air: they neither sow nor
reap nor gather into barns, and yet your heavenly
Father feeds them. Are you not of more value than
they? And which of you by being anxious can add
a single hour to his span of life? And why are you
anxious about clothing? Consider the lilies of the
field, how they grow: they neither toil nor spin,
yet I tell you, even Solomon in all his glory was not
arrayed like one of these. But if God so clothes the
grass of the field, which today is alive and tomorrow is thrown into the oven, will He not much more
clothe you, O you of little faith? Therefore do not be
anxious, saying, "What shall we eat?" or "What shall
we drink?" or "What shall we wear?" For the Gentiles seek after all these things, and your heavenly
Father knows that you need them all. But seek first
the kingdom of God and His righteousness, and all
these things will be added to you.
Therefore do not be anxious about tomorrow, for
tomorrow will be anxious for itself. Sufficient for the
day is its own trouble. (Matthew 6:25–34)

Several things in this passage lead me to conclude that
worry is a waste of time. For instance, I cannot change the
outcome of my life by merely worrying about it. What incredible comfort to know that when I wander into worry,

God forgives me through Christ; He watches over me, caring for my every need. God clothes the lilies of the field and the lilies of my backyard, and I can tell you from firsthand experience that they are definitely dressed in splendor. Since we see evidence of this, then how much more does God know and care for all of my needs! As I step out in obedience, by His grace, I can trust that He has everything under control. He is faithful. Period. He gives me the desire to seek His kingdom and righteousness *first* and the ability to trust that everything else will fall into place.

Earlier in the same sermon, as the Lord taught His people to pray, He included the petition "Give us this day our daily bread" (6:11), revealing God's daily provision for our lives. We need not worry about tomorrow, because we can live only one day at a time. Because we have faith in Him, we live each day under His grace and care, asking for and receiving God's good gifts of today. We can turn tomorrow's worries over to the Lord, who already has tomorrow under control.

Antidotes for Worry

"What works when you're worrying?" a friend asked me, seeking counsel for her own anxiety. My answer: "My Lord works when I am worrying!" Praise Him! Breaking my habit of worry is an ongoing process for me. Along the way, I've learned that He enables me to do a few things, in His strength:

• **Review.** When I begin to worry, I look back at where I have been. I recall the prayers that my heavenly Father, who knows my every need and gives abundantly, has answered in both obvious and subtle ways and often in unexpected ways. I look back to His past provision and of what I've prayed for and for so much more. As I remember with a thankful heart, I am humbled to see how God has used each life detail—the good, the bad, and the ugly—for my good or for the good of some-one else. Thanksgiving is a soothing balm for all that worries me. I find that writing out my prayer list helps. As I return to the list again and again, I record the answers He has given, and I am filled with thanksgiving and praise!

• **Pray.** How often do I lie awake with worry, stewing over the day behind me and the many ways I messed up, or stressing over the day to come and all I have to do? Worry turns to panic. I am learning to take my worry to God when I find myself awake at 4 a.m. because worry is attacking my tranquility. The Lord has led me to cry out to Him as I lie there: "Lord, is this something I am supposed to wrestle through, with Your help?" I articulate my anxiet-ies to Him and ask Him to direct me: "Are You and I to work through this to an action item or insight, or is this just idle worry that I need to let go of? Please make this clear to me. Guide me in Your Word." I whisper, "Lord, You warn me not to worry, but here I go again! In Mat-thew 6, You tell me that You have everything under control. I praise You, for You embrace me and cover me with Your grace, even when I am trapped in worry. You take away my worry and give me sweet rest." "If you lie down, you will not be afraid; when you lie down, your sleep will be sweet" (Proverbs 3:24).

♡ you girl! Courtney Burns

- **Unload.** My daughter, Courtney, shares my predisposition toward worry. Recently, she told me, "Sometimes worry hits me really hard and almost chokes me, like I'm so stressed out that I can't make myself get up and do anything about it." One day in particular, anxiety hit her really hard. It bugged her all day, and she was still feeling heavily burdened by it the next. In her Bible readings, Courtney happened to be reading through Philippians, and that very night she was set to read chapter 4. When she reached verses 6–7, she read, "Do not be anxious about anything, but in everything by prayer and supplication with thanksgiving let your requests be made known to God. And the peace of God, which surpasses all understanding, will guard your hearts and your minds in Christ Jesus." Courtney said, "Obviously, it was a total God-thing that I came across those verses on *that* day, and I knew He was trying to tell me something. I hadn't really prayed about it before, except with maybe a weak, 'God, I hate this anxiety,' so this time I prayed all-out." Courtney unloaded everything that was worrying her, everything that was weighing her down; she laid each thing before the Lord, one at a time.

"And I don't know how soon it was afterward, but I realized that I felt free. All the weight of my anxiety was lifted off my back. God took it all away. I have never seen such a direct, tangible result of prayer before." Whenever the worry or anxiety comes back (and unfortunately, it does), she prays about it just as she did then. And while she doesn't always feel the same degree of freedom, she knows by God's grace that she is indeed free. She trusts that God is in control.

• **Release.** Similarly, when I am feeling anxious, I find it helpful to jot down my worries and physically lay that list aside, envisioning, as I do, that I am laying down my anxiety and worry right at the Lord's feet. As I pray, I give it to Jesus. "Casting all your anxieties on Him, because He cares for you" (1 Peter 5:7). Imagine that! As a fisherman casts his net, throwing it far out into the water, I can pray, throwing my cares out to God and letting go of them. (I must confess: I have a tendency to grab hold of my cares again. It's a good thing I have a God of grace! I can keep giving my cares to Him, time and time again.) As I cast my anxiety out to God—as I trust in Him, by the mighty Spirit's power—He replaces my anxiety with His peace. Peace beyond anything I can comprehend. I, too, look to Philippians 4:6–7 to hear this promise of peace.

A Stepping-Out Story

Far from their roots in the Midwest, Lois and Tom followed the Lord's lead to California when they answered the call to teach in a Lutheran school. After several joy-filled years of service, they were hit with sudden and shocking news: the school would be closing. Although it was only October, the decision was made to finish the school year, and then the doors would be shut for good. Reality set in. That meant uncertainty, unrest, and unemployment.

For months, Lois wrestled over what to do. She struggled with worry. She and Tom cried out in prayer, but she continued to fret. She couldn't imagine what they would do next. Should they remain in California and look for work nearby? Should they return to the Midwest with their preteen son in tow? Months went by with no solid job offers, no clear direction, no prospective calls to ministry. "While we thought nothing was happening to solve our dilemma, God was orchestrating all of His details for us in His perfect timing. All while we sat and stewed." In the midst of her worry, as she saw no evidence of future provision, Lois couldn't perceive how God was working on their behalf. Looking back today, Lois can say with a big smile, "God had already answered our prayer; we just hadn't seen the answer yet."

A month after the end of the school year, as they received their final paychecks, Lois and Tom received an out-of-the-blue phone call from a pastor in Wisconsin, asking if Tom would be interested in a call to teach in their Lutheran Day School. In God's perfect timing, He revealed His plan and provision for their lives. With great joy and relief, they accepted the call.

A surprise bonus to this God-directed plan was that Lois's elderly parents had recently moved to a town just five miles from their new congregation. As her parents' health declined, Lois and Tom were able to minister to them in their final years—an incredible blessing to everyone as many prayers were answered.

Lois was humbly reminded that she need not worry, despite uncertain circumstances or her inability to control a situation. Then, as today, she asks for increased faith, trust, and patience in every circumstance. With wisdom gained through years of practice, learning over and over to trust the Lord, Lois shares, "Even in the midst of our worry, we can't underestimate all the arrangements God is making for us." By God's grace, Lois is stepping out of worry to a place of trust and peace.

God is divinely intervening in your life. He is working on your behalf, even when you cannot see His hand at work. As you look back on His faithful provision, you can cry with the psalmist: "Come and see what God has done: He is awesome in His deeds toward the children of man" (Psalm 66:5). He is awesome in His deeds toward you!

Another Stepping-Out Story
(because worry takes many forms)

I met Elizabeth when her oldest child was only five years old. As a mother of little ones, I was intrigued by her the first time she called to invite me to participate in a new mommy ministry. When we finally met face-to-face, I observed as she interacted tenderly and patiently with her small children. There was something different about her. *What was it?* Elizabeth seemed to possess a great deal of peace and calm, even while juggling three small children. Nothing appeared to rattle her. In contrast, I felt like a walking ball of anxiety as a young mom.

Elizabeth taught me a lot about trust as we each raised our own children, first as neighbors, then from across the country as we kept close ties. Perhaps the reason she was such a good teacher over the years was because she, too, had been a worrier, and while she was still a work-in-progress when I met her, she had sought much strength from the Lord and continued to step out, by the mighty Spirit's power, from a world of worry to a place of trust. She has shared her "worry story" with me.

When Elizabeth was expecting her first child, she was elated. So excited to be pregnant; so eager to bring a baby into the world and begin a family with her husband. Early in the pregnancy, however, worries began to seize her. *Would the baby be healthy? Could she carry the baby to term? Would the delivery be safe?* When her healthy baby boy was born, instead of breathing a great sigh of relief, Elizabeth's worries only worsened: *Would he remain healthy? Would he learn and develop normally?* Her thoughts raced forward, adding to her anxiety: *Would he grow to love the Lord? Would he have friends in kindergarten? Would he give in to peer pressure in high school?* Worry hit her like a tidal wave, and her precious son was barely a month old!

Just as worry threatened to spiral out of control, Elizabeth received a nudge from the Holy Spirit that she should take all her worries to God—every single one of them. (Yes, even her anxious thoughts about high school.) This was the answer to her anxiety and worry. Elizabeth knew that she was capable of protecting her baby boy only to a certain degree. She understood that she and her husband had been entrusted with their baby's care, and that God was and is capable of complete and perfect protection. The Lord knew everything about her son. He knew his future; He was with him wherever he went; He would always take care of him. Elizabeth shared, "One of my consistent prayers was that my son would be healthy spiritually, socially, and academically in high school. Some days I would pray about each one specifically and with more depth. Through these prayers, God gave me peace beyond my own understanding." (Sound familiar? Check out Philippians 4:6–7 *again!*)

As Elizabeth studied God's Word, she was repeatedly reminded that God knows her better than she knows herself. She prayed for herself as a mother, that she would be there for her son even when she didn't know what he needed. "Prayer was my answer for worry. Not only taking to the Lord every worry I had, but also trusting in Him for every detail." She held fast to God's truth as found in one of her favorite verses: "Trust in the LORD with all your heart, and do not lean on your own understanding" (Proverbs 3:5). Although she wouldn't always know or understand the Lord's plans for her son's future, Elizabeth continued to take her worries to the Lord. She laid them before her Savior, and He exchanged them for an unwavering trust in Him.

The years have flown by, and the Lord has richly blessed Elizabeth and her husband as they have sought the Lord's lead and guidance, raising all their children in a faith-filled home. Her son has since graduated from high school. Elizabeth excitedly told me, "I read an entry from a friend in his yearbook that brought tears to my eyes: 'You are such an inspiration: spiritually, socially, and academically.' I knew that many of my prayers have been answered over the years, but to read my very prayer for my son from a high school classmate was an amazing message from God!"

Life on the Edge

What might edgy living without idle worry look like? Again, let's envision moving away from the safe cement behind our beloved diving board, away from the place where we are often overcome with angst and wading in worry. Our Savior extends His hand and bids us to cast our cares—all of them—upon Him. Worry free, we can step up onto the platform, then tiptoe all the way out to the edge, trusting Him all the way, moving forward only because He enables us to take each tiny step.

We are not promised we will be free of trouble or tribulation in this life. In fact, Jesus promises us just the opposite (John 16:33). If we have not faced trials yet, we can know they are coming. My own attempts to find peace from anxiety and worry in the midst of trials are futile. I cannot conjure up my own strength to combat worry with any lasting effect, because my efforts depend on my level of control over the circumstances. But God grants me peace despite the circumstances; He grants me peace although I have little to no control over most situations (even when I pretend that I do!).

Living on the edge means I no longer want to say, "What if?" Instead, I am compelled to shout, "No matter what!" He is my peace, no matter what! I don't know the future, but I am in the grip of the One who does. So no matter what happens, I know He holds me close and gives me peace as only He can. He can take anxiety and worry from me and replace them with a grounded trust in Him, enabling me to continually step out of my worries to a life on the edge.

Life on the edge doesn't mean I will never know worry again. My Savior knows I will struggle; I may take backward steps now and again, maybe even daily, and allow anxiety to grab hold and make me stumble. But my Savior steadies me, moving me forward once more. He fills me with trust that is so much greater than my greatest worries. By the power of Christ, I live on the edge, and I can step out of my worries to a place of trust and peace.

Reflections

1. Look back to past worries and uncertain circumstances. How did things turn out? How did God provide, and how did He use that situation to grow your trust in Him?

2. What worries make you wander like my little sister's senseless sheep? Ask God to help you identify your present worries.

3. Study Matthew 6:25–34. As you do, slip your feet into the sandals of a worried woman in the crowd, seated on the mountainside that day and listening as Jesus spoke these words with great tenderness. Know that He whispers these words to you today. Which verse(s) do you most need to hear right now?

4. Earlier in the chapter, I encouraged you to "look to His promises regarding His continual protection and provision, His presence and His peace." Read Psalm 18:2; Philippians 4:19; Deuteronomy 31:8; Matthew 28:20; and Romans 5:1. Find the Lord's promises in these verses and post a favorite in a prominent place as a continual reminder.

5. Practice jotting down your worries and then physically laying them aside. As you do, envision that you are laying down your anxiety and worry right at the Lord's feet. Pray, giving them all to Jesus; He trades them for His peace.

6. How might the Lord be working on your behalf, in the midst of your most worrisome situation?

7. What might your life on the edge look like as you step out of worry by the Spirit's power into a place of trust, where Christ would have you live?

Write further
reflections here

CHAPTER FOUR

Stepping Out of My Insecurity to a Life of Confidence in Christ

Lies . . .

A voice inside me whispered lies. It told me I didn't have what it takes to accomplish the very thing to which I believe God had been calling me. If I had listened to the lies, I could have become paralyzed by what I perceived to be my limitations. That was insecurity talking. (And when insecurity talks, it never has anything nice to say.)

"Who do you think you are, attempting to lead ministry among those who are old enough to be your mother?"

"They will ask deep theological questions that you can't answer, and then everyone will laugh in your face."

"You know that you are not formally trained as a speaker. You don't belong here."

These destructive whispers and others roared through my

head in the minutes just prior to my leading a women's retreat. You can understand what a stressful time it was, but can you imagine how many insecure thoughts regularly attack me in the span of an average day?

Like every other topic in this book, insecurity is something I struggle with too. If insecurity speaks to you, what lies do you hear? Perhaps they have to do with your relationships or your career. Maybe they are connected to your abilities and gifts, or your perceived lack of them. Or maybe they are related to your appearance or your accomplishments. Perhaps your insecurities are a combination of several of these. Do they start with words such as "You will never be good enough to . . ." or "You are lousy at . . ." or "You don't belong because . . ."? Maybe they try to tell you, "You're not very pretty next to . . ." or "You have to admit that you are lacking in . . ." or "You're just not confident enough to . . ."

Maybe the lies you hear come from inside your head, or maybe they are thrown at you from others. Someone has flung damaging words your way, and you have not been able to dodge them. That person's flawed view of you has left a bruise. Satan loves to use such lies to discourage us and deem us ineffective.

Trapped by insecurity, we may stop in our tracks instead of stepping out to serve, lead, or give, because we are convinced that we don't have enough of the right skill or ability—or we aren't good enough—for God to work with in order to accomplish His purposes. Any one of the following things can leave us thinking we are lacking:

- Limited financial resources

- Lack of talent

- Insufficient training or education

- Limited mobility or declining health

- A history of past failures or perceived failures

- Lack of employment or underemployment

Jesus Steps In

The enemy is intent on filling our minds with destructive thoughts, redirecting our focus to what we may be lacking, what we don't have to offer, and how we are completely insufficient. He seeks to convince us of our failings, either through our own negative beliefs about ourselves or through others' critical words or actions against us.

Then Jesus steps in! He forgives us for falling so easily for Satan's lies, for the lies that caused us to sink into the depths of insecurity. He lifts us out of those depths so we may look to Him, our All-Sufficiency, who so richly provides all that we do have to offer—which is more than enough for Him to accomplish His purposes through us! "Such is the confidence that we have through Christ toward God. Not that we are sufficient in ourselves to claim anything as coming from us, but our sufficiency is from God" (2 Corinthians 3:4–5).

Ephesians 2:10 tells us that we were handcrafted by God. He created us uniquely and individually for the good works He prepared in advance for us to do. Remember this: He gives you exactly what you need to complete exactly the tasks He has in mind for you.

- Maybe what you have to offer is your time or your creativity; your head for numbers or your gift of hospitality; your love of children or your passion for the elderly. The list goes on. And your list is like no other.

- You have something special to offer, regardless of the level of worldly training you have received.

- God will use whatever financial resources—small or large—that you offer in faith to extend His kingdom through the Church, the mission field, or the community, however and wherever He leads you to give.

- You have a unique purpose, according to God's plan, even if your health is failing and regardless of past failures. He gives you His grace, which enables you to pick up your feet and step out to try once again.

Take a look at all you *do* have to offer. Maybe you can't sing or dance, but you can teach teens about Jesus. Maybe you aren't comfortable speaking in public, but people are still talking about the yummy cherry cheesecake you made for the new pastor's installation dinner. Maybe you have a knack with the very young or the very old, or you are a whiz at spreadsheets and the role of church treasurer appeals to you. These are gifts of God to be used for His glory. Isn't that exciting?

Ignited by the spark of the Spirit, a fire grows in our hearts for the task right in front of us. Led by the Lord, we step out of that insecure place into one where we are emboldened to serve Him with confidence, not the so-called self-confidence the world speaks of, but God confidence, which is incomparably greater! We are confident not because we think we have all that it takes, but because we know the One who does. We know the One who is working in and through us to accomplish His perfect plans. "God is able to make all grace abound to you, so that having all sufficiency in all things at all times, you may abound in every good work" (2 Corinthians 9:8). By His grace, He takes the little we have and uses it for His big, beautiful purposes, as only He can. He says we are sufficient, lacking nothing, to accomplish every good work that He may be glorified in it.

"Now to Him who is able to do far more abundantly than all that we ask or think, according to the power at work within us, to Him be glory in the church and in Christ Jesus" (Ephesians 3:20–21). Did you catch that? By His power at work within you, He is able to do so much more *in* and *through* you than you can even think to ask Him for!

Let the Holy Spirit lead you to God's Word of truth. This is where you will be affirmed of your God-given abilities; this is where you can seek real security. When your lack of confidence says, "I can't do anything," Jesus' Word says, "I can do all things through Him who strengthens me" (Philippians 4:13).

- Are you ready for a few more examples of the truth about you?

- You are so dearly loved, that God Himself calls you His child (1 John 3:1).

- You are specifically chosen by God; you belong to Him (1 Peter 2:9).

- You are so valuable that you were bought with a great price (1 Corinthians 7:23).

- The Lord lavishes His grace upon you, forgiving you for all your sins (Ephesians 1:7–8).

- You have been saved by grace through faith; this is God's gift to you (Ephesians 2:8–9).

As His Word of truth fills us, the lies are forced out. Our insecurity diminishes as we focus on how God thinks of us instead of on how we think of ourselves or how others think of us.

A Journey through Insecurity

Throughout Linda's high school years, she saw only a very distorted view of herself. Like many of us during our tumultuous teens, Linda struggled with insecurity. Her family members seemed so accomplished, and she felt so inadequate next to them. Although they saw great potential in her, she could not see it in herself.

Linda's distorted self-perception had taken root when she was in grade school. During those formative years, she was a shy bookworm, she was chubby, and she was certainly not an athlete. Her self-perception was further distorted by the reaction of her peers, especially the girls, who were not accepting of her. To make matters worse, she was a pastor's kid in a rough congregation. Parents used Linda as an example to their own children of how a "good" kid should behave. You can imagine how other children reacted to that! How many strikes against her could there be?

A move from a rural area to suburban Chicago just before high school compounded Linda's problems. She sank into depression and suffered from school phobia. She was a mess. "Even if I had heard positive words, I wouldn't have really 'heard' them," she says. During those trying years, Linda was able to receive Christian counseling and much-needed love and support from her family, all of whom God used to help Linda see her real value and worth and begin to recognize her identity in Him.

Bit by bit, God revealed Linda's gifts to her, and then He provided opportunities for her to use them—first, a gift for music, then a passion for teaching, and still later a knack for leadership. As she became aware of these God-given gifts, she developed confidence to try new things, to discover new talents, to unpack the gifts He had already custom-created in her. (Take another peek at Ephesians 2:10.)

Linda smiles broadly now. "Through counseling and life experience," she says, "God turned that 'mess' into a leader. The journey from insecurity to competence was a faith journey where God used seemingly unrelated gifts and worked them together for His purpose." By God's grace, Linda was able to step out of a dark place of insecurity and into His marvelous light, secure with confidence in Him. "Our lives are filled with continual discovery; it's an adventure to realize what gifts He has given us and the value in them!"

Although some of Linda's insecurity came from her own distorted, negative thoughts of herself, a good portion was pushed on her by those who excluded her or disapproved of her. Her perception of herself, combined with others' treatment of her, caused her to feel inadequate. I wonder if, to some degree, that is how the bleeding woman in Mark 5:25–34 felt. This woman, marked unclean by her peers and by her religious leaders, had every reason to feel insecure. Excluded. Disapproved. Rejected. Although the cause may have been quite different from Linda's or ours, her resulting insecurity may have been much the same.

Slip your feet into her sandals and witness a life-changing encounter with Jesus through her eyes.

Healed!

Pain. Humiliation. Exclusion. Were these the feelings that drew her there, into the crowd, to the Teacher? The risk was great, she knew. Would someone recognize her and shout, "Unclean!"? Desperation led her to go anyway. Desperation and hope.

For twelve years, uncontrolled bleeding had made her unclean. Twelve long years of suffering, of being shunned by her community and cast away from her family, of feeling lonely and insecure. According to the law, if she were to even touch another person, she could be charged with defiling that person. Even the chair she sat on and pallet that was her bed were unclean. She had tried everything, every known cure. The doctors had no solution for her. She had spent all of her money on treatments. All her options were gone. And still the bleeding continued.

Then she heard about Him. Jesus. People said He was healing the sick. They said He was performing miracles. And a miracle was what she needed.

She believed that this Healer—this Miracle Worker—could make her well again, so she took the risk. She made her way into the crowd. There were so many people pushing and straining toward Jesus, pressing against Him. Some called out, "Master!" Others cried, "Teacher, heal me!" *So many people in pain. Could they be as desperate as I am?* she thought. She squeezed past the others to approach Him from behind. She bent low and hid her face in her cloak. She knew that if she could just touch Him, if she could reach far enough to feel the hem of His robe—even just the fringe of His garment—she would be healed. She reached out her hand, and then something indescribable happened. Just as the tips of her fingers touched the edge of His robe, her body felt immediately different. Miraculously, the bleeding stopped. She was healed!

Although the crowds still pressed around Him on every side, Jesus abruptly stopped and stood still. He turned around, a knowing expression on His face. "Who touched My garments?" He asked. His closest followers shook their heads in confusion at His question, stating what appeared to be obvious: "You see the crowd pressing around You, and yet You say, 'Who touched Me?'" (Mark 5:30, 31).

The woman was terrified, too insecure to answer. She was afraid to admit what she'd done and be the center of condemnation. After all, everyone knew she was unclean. With her in their midst, they'd all be unclean too. Not only that, but by her touch, she had also defiled the Teacher. But it was obvious that He knew it was she. It was clear that He knew she was the one who had reached out in desperate hope and touched the hem of His robe. She could no longer hide.

Trembling, she approached Jesus and fell at His feet. Everyone in the crowd stared as she spoke. She told Jesus the whole truth—why she had touched Him and how she had been healed instantly. Jesus, unlike the crowd, looked on her with compassionate love. "Daughter, your faith has made you well; go in peace, and be healed of your disease" (v. 34). Hearing these tender words, the woman knew she had received healing—body and soul—by Jesus' power. His grace covered her and made her whole; she was forgiven and clean! Her desperate risk had been worth every moment of fear and insecurity.

And He called her *daughter,* a beloved child of God and an heir to His kingdom! His words proclaimed to her, and to everyone who heard, that her shame, her sin, and her insecurity were taken away, were replaced by His healing, hope, and mercy. Her confidence was in Christ Jesus, her Healer and Savior.

Are you living with rejection, humiliation, or pain? Or have you seen another person excluded because he or she didn't project a certain image or live up to the standards that society prizes or expects? Perhaps you have never been cast out or called unclean, but you still know the hurt of isolation, the pain of exclusion, the pang of disapproval. Perhaps you suffer from a chronic illness that causes others to recoil. Filled with the Holy Spirit, you can cry out to Jesus. Reach out your hand in confident hope to the One who knows your insecurity and pain and hears your every prayer. Fall at the feet of the One who steps in and fills your loneliness with His presence and His perfect peace. Hear the tender words of the One who gives you your identity and value, claims you as His own dear daughter, and looks on you with compassionate love.

This side of heaven, we may not understand the purpose for our struggles with insecurity or the reason for our pain and rejection, but we can take heart that Jesus, our Savior, provides us with the ultimate healing. Stained by sin, we all are unclean. But our heavenly Healer reaches out in love and washes us with His cleansing grace. We are forgiven, filled with hope and faith! "Daughter, your faith has made you well." We step out in faith, no longer insecure, but confident of our salvation in Christ and secure in Him.

A Stepping-Out Story

Being a mommy was the best! Brooke had given birth three times in four years and was thrilled to have the opportunity to stay home with her children. She was immersed in mommyhood, consumed with every special detail. Even the lack of sleep and the constant care didn't curtail Brooke's joy in raising her children. While she kept her foot in the door at the office, working just one afternoon a week outside the home, her primary career was child-rearing.

Brooke's best friend was also a stay-at-home mom. The two women got together three to four times a week, children in tow. They were both tied down with their little ones and enjoyed their mutual adult conversation while changing diapers, feeding hungry mouths, and fixing boo-boos. Brooke and her best friend bonded as they shared similar life circumstances. Their husbands had comparable careers too, and they even worshiped at the same church. Their children were also good buddies, spending lots of time in each other's homes as the two moms took turns babysitting and providing breaks for each other.

Because being a mommy had been a lifelong dream for Brooke, she stepped into this career with gusto. While she had often struggled with some insecurity, she felt confident and secure in her role as a mother. Brooke's focus was so intent on her children that she let it become her only focus. Sure, she gave some time and attention to her friend because they shared the same passion. But had she done the same for her husband? Was she giving much thought to his needs throughout this time? Looking back, Brooke regrets, "I forgot that before I could be a mother to my children, I first needed to be a wife to my husband. I can see now how I was ignoring his needs. But it was not a conscious decision at the time; I was just so excited and distracted with my mommy role."

She had noticed that her husband was becoming moody and withdrawn; she knew something was wrong. Finally, he confessed to her that he was having feelings of attraction for her best friend. *Her best friend?! What was he saying?!* He had gone so far as to call the friend's home with the excuse of church commitments, just hoping to talk to her. But when he called, her husband answered, so his phone conversation with her never happened. It was shortly after this that he confessed these feelings to Brooke.

Nothing had happened. So why did Brooke feel so awful and so insecure? *Why am I making a big deal of this?* she thought. Maybe it was because she felt emotionally betrayed. Initially, she had feelings of anger toward her husband, then toward herself. Then insecurity hit her really hard: *What does he see in her that he doesn't see in me? What makes her better than me?* Brooke's best friend was a beautiful, thin, blue-eyed blonde. She was so well put together and fun to be around. Did Brooke suffer in comparison? If she felt a little insecure before, her feelings were now compounded tenfold.

Brooke was also feeling isolated because she couldn't share her husband's confession or her resultant insecurities with anyone. Her confidante, her best friend, was the last person in the world she would want to talk to about this, because she was the object of her husband's interest. What would this mean for their friendship?

Brooke's husband had confessed his inappropriate feelings, and he asked for her forgiveness; he reassured her that his love and commitment were only for her. "For better or for worse, . . . until death do us part." And on the surface, they carried on, looking to be a loving, happy couple, a commendable church-going family. But under that facade, Brooke struggled greatly with self-worth and insecurity. "I was insecure about myself, my body, my abilities, my 'fill-in-the-blank,'" she admits.

Brooke confesses that she wasn't as loving and caring of her husband as she could have been during this strained time. She withdrew intimacy, which was the opposite of what he needed. While her husband reassured her over and over that he loved her, she was plagued by doubts and insecure thoughts: *Is he thinking about her when he is with me? What about other women? the pretty secretary at his office?*

About eighteen months after her husband's confession, Brooke attended a work-related professional-training session within a ministry-education group. As the group talked about ministering to people in their pain, Brooke surprised herself by suddenly opening up and spilling her heart about the entire story. It was a safe place to share, as no one in the group knew her husband, and the others could respond in a professional, yet personal, Christian manner. "You are trying to put up a good front, but you need help," they told her gently. As they witnessed her raw emotions, they could see that she showed signs of depression, although she had not been willing to admit them to herself. And when she was diagnosed with depression, feelings of anger surfaced again— she was the one labeled with a "problem," when she felt that her husband was the very reason she was experiencing this dark time and, in contrast, he was getting off scot-free.

Brook attended several sessions with a Christian counselor, first alone and then later with her husband. She laid out all of her feelings, her vulnerabilities and insecurities, before the counselor. Over time, with a great deal of communication, patience, and forgiveness, healing began to happen. Brooke says she can't remember when, exactly, she was able to say, "everything is okay," but eventually, it was. The Lord provided protection and healing for their marriage. He enabled Brooke to step out of her pain and insecurity.

Ecclesiastes 4:12 talks about a cord of three strands not being quickly broken. As Brooke and her husband acknowledge Christ as the third and center strand of their marriage, she shares, "When two strands were fraying, the third was still solid, holding the cord together. He is our strength."

By God's grace, Brooke and her husband came out on the other side of their struggles stronger and closer. To this day, he helps her to see that she is a beautiful child of God— physically, emotionally, and spiritually. "I wish you could see yourself through my eyes," he tells her over and over. He affirms her, even when she doesn't want to hear it.

And God's Word affirms her even more. When insecure thoughts creep in, she hears from the Lord. He has chosen her to be His treasured possession in Christ (Deuteronomy 14:2). She knows that her life is precious in the sight of the Lord (1 Samuel 26:24). She recognizes that she is uniquely created by God, that she is the work of His hands (Psalm 138:8). Brooke says with a smile, "Hearing something over and over makes you finally believe it."

Perhaps at one time, we were confident and secure, wrapping our identity and security around our role of mother, wife, professional, teacher, or the like. Then life changed or something knocked our confidence out from under us, and our world of security came crumbling down. The "stay-at-home mom" no longer had a purpose, because the children all grew up and flew away. The "wife" label didn't apply when there was no husband in the house anymore. The title of "professional" evaporated with a layoff or retirement. And now we are unsure of our self-worth, our abilities, and our very identity. The role in which we found security and confidence is gone, and we are lost.

It is true that our many roles help to define who we are in relationship to others and how we are to serve them. In fact, God blesses us with these relationships and these roles. But if we let our identity rest solely on those roles, we mistakenly think we are without identity when those roles change or go away.

Even when our roles change, we don't change in that we still possess the same abilities, gifts, and talents. Those traits can still be used to glorify God, although they are now meant to be aimed in a new direction. We can ask Him to reveal the next step in His plans for us as they fit into His purposes, and He will empower us to step out, using all we have learned for the new roles that lie ahead. We can trust Him when He reminds us of our value and identity, regardless of our roles. After all, who we are, first and foremost, is really a matter of *whose* we are.

Our most basic and unchanging identity is found and centered in Christ. He has redeemed us; He has called us by name, and we belong to Him. (See Isaiah 43:1.) No matter what happens in life, regardless of how our roles change, our security, value, and confidence do not have to change because they are rooted in Him. Our ultimate security lies in His definition of us. Our confidence comes from trusting the truth that we are who God says we are: forgiven, redeemed daughters of God, chosen in Christ. We are rescued by the Redeemer, who stepped out of the security of heaven and entered this world, fully man yet still fully God, who endured the agony of the cross and died in our place, who conquered the grave and provides for us the eternal security of a home in heaven. Confident in Christ, we are assured of our salvation, which we have received by grace through faith.

Life on the Edge

The devil wears the guise of insecurity. He persists in speaking to me, threatening me until I go to the back of that old diving board, step down, and stay there, trembling in my timid tootsies. But Christ speaks so much more powerfully. He fills me with strength and courage, telling me to trust Him as He takes my hand and leads me to the edge. Jesus is my all-sufficiency, my confidence, and my sure-and-certain hope. In Him, I can do all things! Out here on the edge, He enables me to see what I have to offer and how He may use me to accomplish His purposes. How exciting is that? I pray that He would continue to reveal to me the gifts He has given me and is growing in me. He gives me the confidence to step out; to lead, serve, and give to others with the best of my God-given abilities.

Back behind the diving board, quaking in our insecurity, we may have thought that we had nothing to offer others, but we have, in fact, the greatest gift of all to share: the very gift of God, given to us in Christ Jesus! As we step out of our insecurity to a life on the edge, prompted by the One who is our security and our confidence, we give others the Good News of eternal life in Christ.

Reflections

1. When insecurity speaks to you, what lies do you hear? Are they connected to your relationships, your career, or your perception of your abilities and gifts? Let God lead you to His Word of truth to combat those lies. Find a promise to replace each lie. (If you would like, begin with those I've shared throughout this chapter.)

2. Read Matthew 9:20–22; Mark 5:25–34; and Luke 8:42–48, three parallel passages that narrate the bleeding woman's encounter with Christ. Once again, place your feet in her sandals while you read. Imagine what went through her mind as Jesus called her "daughter" and told her that her faith had made her well. Beyond physical healing, how do you think her life was changed from that moment on?

3. Which of your current roles give definition to your life today (e.g., girlfriend, wife, teacher)? List some past roles that no longer define you (e.g., student, clerk, stay-at-home mom). During your times of transition, did you feel a temporary loss of identity? Explain.

4. What unchanging roles define you (e.g., child of your parents, child of God in Christ, redeemed)? Post some of these in a prominent place for continual reminders.

5. Read again 2 Corinthians 3:4–5 and 9:8. Both passages speak of sufficiency. How would you define this word, and how do you know that you are sufficient to carry out your roles and complete the tasks God has for you?

6. Write the first positive word that comes to mind concerning your personality, character traits, talents and gifts, learned skills, appearance. No other list looks like yours. The Creator made you uniquely special. Your identity and security are found in none other than Jesus Himself!

7. What might your life on the edge look like as, by the power of the Spirit, you step out of your insecurity to a place of confidence in Christ?

Write further
reflections here

CHAPTER FIVE

Stepping Out of My Need to Please to a Life Lived for an Audience of One

May I Please You? Pretty Please?

I lie awake, rehashing conversations and interactions in my mind. Most of time, I rehash recent interactions, but sometimes I relive conversations from months or even years ago:

> "I talked too much—again—and I think she was in a hurry to go. She probably won't stop by anymore, for fear I will never let her leave."
> *Translation:* "What if my **many** words were not pleasing to her?"

"They probably think I'm a snob because I barely
spoke to them at church when we visited.
But the truth is that I just wasn't feeling well."
Translation: "What if my **lack** of words was
not pleasing to them?"

"Did I give her enough attention during the break
time at last year's women's retreat? Oh, dear, I hope
I said the right things to encourage her, but what
if she misunderstood what I was trying to say?"
Translation: "What if my **words**, in general, did not
please her?"

"I'm sure the neighbor thinks I don't like dogs
because he heard me yelling at Tanner again."
(Tanner is our hyperactive Brittany spaniel,
for whom I have little patience.) "He probably
thinks I yell at my husband and kids the
way I bark at my pooch!"
Translation: "What if my **choice** of words
were misunderstood?"

If I feel this strongly about what my neighbor thinks regarding my relationship with my dog, then you can probably imagine the angst I feel over those other matters—the
situations in which I actually had to interact with people
face-to-face.

I have been known to pretend to like something just to fit
in. "I just, er, uh, *love* that movie genre. You want to watch
it now? *Oh boy.* Can't wait!" I even choose activities based

on what I think others want me to do: "Coed softball? Sure, count me in! That's my kind of sport!" (Wait until they find out I can't hit or catch to save myself.)

Seeking the Approval of . . . Everyone!

I have a deep hunger to be affirmed, accepted, loved. I want everyone in a thousand-mile radius to not only like me but to also like what I accomplish, to give me a firm nod of approval, and not to stop there. I imagine words of affirmation coming my way: "Deb, I like what you've done with your hair." "Honey, you certainly are doing a great job of *(insert one of hundreds of possibilities here)."* "You are so friendly; I wish there were more people like you." (Hmm, it appears this chapter might overlap with a following chapter about pride!) Just call me Words-of-Affirmation Woman. My closest family members do. They know I crave an "atta girl" and "good job" for just about everything I say and do, not to mention for how I look. (Is this also a chapter about vanity?)

While positive, affirming words are a beneficial and healthy way to give and receive encouragement, I tend to take it too far in my quest for approval. I quickly judge my "performance"—everything from the meal I just made to the Bible study I led to the volunteer work I did by the words or reactions, judgment or opinion of other people, not by how I felt about it or by the simple satisfaction of a job done faithfully to the glory of God. If I do not meet their "approval," I feel instantly rejected; I feel like less of a person; I think I have failed.

Wait—you're a people-pleaser too? You also have a need for approval, a desire to be liked?

"No Matter What You Do . . ."

For people-pleasers, these are some of the most difficult words to hear: "No matter what you do, not everyone is going to like you." This is a common response; perhaps you have heard it too. I think the first time I heard these wise words, they came from my father as he responded to his teary-eyed daughter—me—who sat in the backseat of the car blubbering about another eighth grader who had bullied me that day. You see, I had wanted so badly for this girl to like me. When our little country schools came together for special events, she was always the social butterfly of the group, fluttering about gracefully, receiving all kinds of attention. She was one of those pretty, popular types that everyone liked. (Did you catch that? *Everyone* liked her.) On that particular day, for whatever reason, she let everyone else know that they should *not* like *me*. What was wrong with me? What could I have done differently? Should I have tried harder? Was it my appearance or my personality?

"No matter what you do, Debbie, not everyone is going to like you." From the driver's seat, my father gave me this basic counsel that sticks to this day, although I continue to struggle in my desire for approval. This reality, this basic truth, is difficult to receive by anyone who refers to herself as a "pleaser." If you fall into this category, then you know what I mean. We are terrified at the thought of other people being angry or upset with us. And even if we are assured that someone likes us, we fret that he or she won't approve of every little thing we do. We may even place conditions on their relationship, supposing that if we cease to please the person, the friendship and love will somehow cease.

This is ridiculous thinking, perhaps, but such are the secret thoughts of a pleaser.

Our Audience

What drives us to do what we do? Do we analyze our words, our actions, and our every effort in connection with our boyfriend or husband? our parents? our children? members of our church? our neighbors? our co-workers? our latest acquaintances? There is an entire audience of people whom we believe is watching our every move. Sometimes, we try to please everyone, even the checker at the grocery store. If our motives as we serve any one of these individuals or an entire audience are merely to gain their acceptance, their accolades, and even their applause, then we are serving for the wrong reasons. We are judging ourselves and even our self-worth on how we interpret other people's often-shifting opinions of our performance. And as we do, we are making our service all about us.

In an effort to please, do we ever allow our words or actions to go against our Christian convictions? Take for instance a time when the conversation turned into gossip and we failed to squelch it for fear that we would meet the disapproval of someone in the room. Or what about when we chose to read a popular book that we knew contained an unwholesome message, because everyone else was talking about it in their social networks? Perhaps we have given in to premarital sex just to please the man we thought was Mr. Right. Maybe we caved to peer pressure and engaged in illegal behavior just to look good to our friends. The truth is that many of us have struggled to stand firm in our convictions when they were not part of the popular stance for fear that our relationships or our reputation will be ruined if we lost the approval of a mass audience.

Jesus Steps In

How I long to step out from under this heavy burden, this unhealthy need to please, this desire for constant and complete approval of everyone. But I cannot do it alone. On my own, the only steps I seem to take are a sort of sheepish shuffling toward those people from whom I think I need approval.

Then Jesus steps in and onto the scene. He forgives me for my messed-up motives and my wrong reasons for serving. He redeems me from my desire to please others instead of seeking to please Him. He and He alone can take me by the hand and spin me around, sending me in His direction, moving me to step out and away from my unhealthy need for people's approval and toward a life lived solely for Him.

What about God's approval? How do we earn it? Brace yourself for this truth: we already have it!

"This is my beloved Son, with whom I am well *pleased"* (Matthew 3:17, emphasis added). At Jesus' Baptism, the voice of the Lord came from heaven, announcing His perfect approval of His Son, who was beginning His public ministry. Because Jesus the man kept His focus on God's purpose, He was willing to step out in faith and do His earthly work. Ultimately, God's Son would suffer and die for our sins and, because of that, release us from our unhealthy desire to seek others' approval. The result of Jesus' work is that now we have our Lord's approval—not because of anything we say or do, not because of who our parents were or what our children do, and not because of our appearance or performance. We can't buy it and we can't earn it. No attempt to please God on our own can ever be good enough.

We cannot find God's approval outside of Christ. When God looks at us, He sees us through Christ. Christ's perfection covers us, and God smiles down on us, His chosen and adopted children. Because of Christ, God says to us, "I am well pleased." By His glorious grace, and His limitless love, we live our lives for an audience of One—the One who gave His life for us.

When Jesus stepped into the lives of the people of Israel, bringing a message of faith and forgiveness, He did so not to please them but only to obey and glorify His Father. "I do nothing on My own authority, but speak just as the Father taught Me. And He who sent Me is with Me. He has not left Me alone, for I always do the things that are pleasing to Him" (John 8:28–29).

Jesus taught "as one who had authority" (Mark 1:22), and His teachings of grace about the kingdom of God threatened the authority of the religious rulers and the long-standing laws they lorded over the people. (These rulers—the Pharisees, the Sadducees and the teachers of the law—did not like Jesus one bit!) Jesus healed on the Sabbath, a big no-no, according to the legalistic interpretation of the law. He associated with sinners and those who were considered unclean by the law. The religious leaders closed their ears to His truth, to His perfect fulfillment of the messianic prophecies.

They were threatened by His authority and jealous of His popularity, and they wanted Him dead. Did any of this stop Jesus from doing and saying that which was pleasing to the Father and was according to His will? Of course not, because Jesus, the sinless Son of God, was focused only on obedience to the Father. Despite what others thought of Him, Jesus continued

- speaking just as the Father taught Him;

- doing only what was pleasing to the Father; and

- trusting that the Father was right by His side.

There was no wiggle room for people-pleasing in Jesus' walk. His God-pleasing journey took Him all the way to the cross. And when He was charged, tried, convicted, ridiculed, tortured, and crucified, His enemies believed they had gotten their way. What they failed to see was that it was the will of our loving heavenly Father that His sinless Son should suffer and die. What they failed to see was that He suffered in the place of those who could not perfectly keep the Law and obey Him on their own.

He died for us because we fail to speak as He has taught us in His Word.

He suffered for us because we busily try to please other people.

He gave His life for us because we do so much that is not pleasing to Him.

Despite our many failures, our Father remains by our side, forgives us for Jesus' sake, and gives us the courage and ability to live for Him and with confidence that we have His approval in Christ.

We Have Been with Jesus!

In the earliest days of the Church, as recorded in Acts 3–4, the apostles Peter and John healed a crippled man in the name and power of Jesus Christ. Crowds gathered in amazement, and Peter began to teach them. As a result, he and John met with strong disapproval of the Jewish leaders—the same group that had condemned Jesus. The two apostles were seized and jailed overnight. The next day, they were brought for questioning before the priests, rulers, and teachers of the law.

With power and boldness, unafraid of what the religious authorities thought of him, Peter proclaimed salvation in Christ alone. His accusers were astonished. They recognized Peter and John to be ordinary, unschooled men who were not authorized to teach, and they realized that they had been with Jesus. Peter cried out against the Jewish leaders, who now threatened to silence him and all the apostles by forbidding them to speak the name of Jesus. Filled with the power of the Spirit, Peter cried, "For we cannot but speak of what we have seen and heard" (Acts 4:20).

This was the same Peter who had crumbled in fear and timidity on earlier occasions, sinking amid the wind and waves as he attempted to walk on water and denying Jesus when confronted during His trial. (Was Peter a pleaser like me?) Peter was changed by being with Jesus, and he could not be silent about the saving Gospel message. With the authority of Christ now at work in him, Peter was no longer afraid of his adversaries, and he was not looking for their approval. He stepped out in faith, boldly proclaiming salvation in Jesus' name by the power of the Holy Spirit. Peter was prepared to give an answer before his critics and accusers—because he had been with Jesus.

If I were to place my timid tootsies in the apostle Peter's sturdy sandals, would I step out with conviction, standing firm for the truth of Christ in the face of persecution or death? Or would I slink back sheepishly, apologizing for having offended the authorities, pitifully promising never to do *that* again because it displeased them so? I pray that I would be so bold, strengthened by faith in the Savior, to step out as Peter did, despite opposition and regardless of the response—because I have been with Jesus.

The Holy Spirit later inspired Peter to write these words: "Always [be] prepared to make a defense to anyone who asks you for a reason for the hope that is in you" (1 Peter 3:15). The Lord gives us the desire to grow in His Word. He prepares us for every challenge and fills us with courage. Because Jesus is with us, we—like Peter—are changed too. We no longer have the need to seek the approval of an unbelieving and critical world. Instead, we are confident that we have God's approval in Christ. He fuels us with words and abilities that are clearly His and not our own. Like Peter and John, we cannot keep Him to ourselves; we are inspired to step out with joy and shout His praises to the world. He is in our hearts and on our lips!

A Stepping-Out Story

A mother of elementary-age children, Kris was a Christian woman whose greatest desire was to see her brood continue to grow in their baptismal faith and in their love and knowledge of their Savior. Kris was thrilled when she and her husband found a Christian school for their children to attend. The faith and values taught in the classrooms mirrored those she and her husband instilled and modeled at home as they relied on the Lord to lead them in their parenting.

Kris jumped in to help in her kids' classrooms and wherever else she was needed. Prayers for her children were answered as she saw them grow academically, spiritually, and socially. While the children were enjoying fun new friendships at school, Kris was actively involved in serving in the church too, and in forming friendships of her own, many with the parents of her children's friends. Kris was well liked by the church staff and the teachers, the parents and the children, partly because she was such a pleaser. "Yes, I was bent on pleasing *everyone,*" Kris sighs, as she tells her story.

Looking back, Kris says, "I loved to serve. I did what I was asked—with a smile. And most of the time, that wasn't a problem. I wanted to make the teachers happy, not to mention the parents with whom I worked alongside." When other parents had differing opinions on certain subjects, Kris kept quiet. She determined that peace was more profitable than conflict. She didn't have a strong opinion about most minor matters anyway; at least none worth making enemies over. In the grand scheme of things, she thought, did it really matter what theme was chosen for a classroom party or what food was served at a youth group event?

Outgoing and friendly, Kris led by example, helping people work together and get along. In children's ministry, during Bible class, on field trips, in the classroom—soon she was taking on larger leadership roles. She had a knack for recognizing others' gifts and encouraging them to get involved too. She made some mistakes along the way and learned quickly that no matter how hard you try, someone may be unhappy with you in your lead role. While that part of leadership was very difficult for Kris, pleaser that she was, the overriding affirmation from her peers was very gratifying. "Oh, Kris, you are such a committed leader." "Wow, Kris, the teachers loved what you did!" "Thanks, Kris, for the way you shared your faith." She knew how good it felt to receive encouragement, so she handed out plenty too.

When her daughter was in middle school, Kris noticed the positive impact of contemporary Christian music on her family. She also was aware of the influence of other types of music, which were not always as positive. This was not an issue in Sunday School or youth group, of course, but Kris could see that many families listened only to secular music, which was not often uplifting. Then children began bringing that secular music into the school.

Then it happened. Kris found herself in a situation where she could not keep quiet. Unlike so many matters over the years, this one was not so trivial. Some of the girls in her daughter's class were to perform a dance routine before an all-school assembly, choreographed by another mother. This was not an area of leadership for Kris, and she knew little about it. But when she was asked to attend a rehearsal, Kris was shocked to hear the song that was chosen and see the dance moves the girls were learning. The song included implicit sexual lyrics, and some of the motions reflected the words all too closely. To make matters worse, the song had been approved by the school staff. Kris was crushed by this news.

"I was faced with a situation where I could not make everyone happy. I could see that my daughter was uncomfortable with the song and dance choices. She didn't want to look like a loser and leave, so she kept practicing." Kris struggled over what to do. Pleaser that she was, it was difficult to consider speaking up. Would she lose some friendships if she dared to share her feelings? What about the mutual respect she shared with the staff? But what kind of witness would this give to the students and their families at the assembly? And what about her daughter? Was peace with these others more important than staying true to their values?

With courage that could have come only from the Lord, Kris stepped out of her need to please and spoke up. She shared her concerns as respectfully as she could, pointing out the lyrics and the motions, reminding the leaders who the audience would be and the Christian witness the school sought to provide. She asked them to please reconsider. Kris says they looked at her as if she had suddenly grown a second nose. A few pointed out that it was their daughters' favorite song. Some responded defensively, claiming that "everyone listens to it anyway, even the younger children." Some merely shrugged, mumbling something about it not being a big deal. Still others looked concerned and nervously shuffled their feet but remained silent. (Perhaps Kris was not the only pleaser in the room.)

Sadly, nothing changed. Kris did not forbid her daughter to participate in the dance routine; she let her decide what to do. The day of the assembly arrived, and the girls on the dance team lined up on the floor—all but Kris's daughter. Where was she? When the music began, Kris turned and saw her daughter sitting quietly in the stands. While the other girls danced, her daughter sat and watched. She joined the group on the floor when the song was over. Afterward, she told her mother, "I just couldn't go through with it." Later, a couple of parents approached Kris to quietly thank her for doing the right thing and for her courage to speak up and take the unpopular position, although it didn't please everyone.

So maybe it isn't true, after all, to say that nothing changed. God used this incident to prick the consciences of several people and encourage others to take a similar stand later (for instance, the staff decided to take a closer look at lyrics in the future). Would this have happened had Kris not stepped out?

Even more important for Kris was the impact this incident had on her daughter. Later that same school year, her daughter wrote a special thank-you note to her. Included in the note were these words: "I really admire the strong faith that you have, and how you stand true to your morals, even when everyone around you doesn't. That inspires me so much, and I want to be like you."

Praise God for the faith He provides through our Savior, Jesus Christ! He gives us the courage to step out for the truth, even when the rest of the world won't. The world is watching our every move, waiting for us Christians to take a misstep. Instead of trying to please the people of the world, may we strive to live in such a way that they see Christ in us and be drawn to Him.

Life on the Edge

Perhaps we will not be persecuted for proclaiming Jesus or standing up for the truth in the same way the apostles were and as millions of Christians around the world are persecuted today. We may, however, be mocked or made fun of, insulted or accused, criticized or cast out when our desire to please Christ triumphs over our need to please our neighbor, friend, or even a family member. (These are more tough words for a people-pleaser to hear!) Jesus foretold that His followers would be hated and hurt, and yes, persecuted, as we live for Him. But when this harsh world sees you and me—former people-pleasers—now boldly proclaiming the name of Christ Jesus and courageously living on the edge for Him, they will be astonished. Perhaps they will even exclaim like Peter's accusers, "She has been with Jesus!" And like Peter, we can be certain that God will use our courageous witness to influence others' lives that they, too, would desire to live for Him.

Not that this is easy. I still need a nudge from the Holy Spirit to step closer to the edge of my comfort zone and live boldly as a Christian witness. Here are a few prayers that I pray as I'm taking those steps:

• I pray for strength to resist focusing on what another person thinks of me, that I not feel the need to live with a vain attempt to please the world around me.

I ask God to help me remember that others' opinions of me, and their words or actions against me, do not define who I am or give measure to my value or worth. I thank Him that in His eyes, I am valuable enough that He sent His Son to give His life for me. And I ask that, with the joy of the Spirit, I can live my life solely for Him. "For if we live, we live to the Lord, and if we die, we die to the Lord. So then, whether we live or whether we die, we are the Lord's" (Romans 14:8).

- "No matter what you do, not everyone is going to like you." While I cannot control the way others respond to me or make them accept my beliefs or convictions, I can pray that God will use my humble witness for His purpose. Even as I do good to other people (because of my response to Jesus, and not merely to please others), I may not be treated well by them. But God always accepts me in Christ, perfectly and fully. Therefore, I pray for a heart for sharing the Gospel, regardless of other people's response. "But just as we have been approved by God to be entrusted with the gospel, so we speak, not to please man, but to please God who tests our hearts" (1 Thessalonians 2:4).

- And I pray that God would prepare me, through the study of His Word, "to make a defense to anyone who asks [me] for a reason for the hope that is in [me]" and that I might do this "with gentleness and respect, having a good conscience, so that, when [I am] slandered, those who revile [my] good behavior in Christ may be put to shame" (1 Peter 3:15–16).

Reflections

1. Has the overriding desire to please others gotten its grip on you? Have you pretended to like something just to fit in? Do you tend to judge your "performance," your every action, based on someone else's judgment of it, or are you more often content with the quality of your work, knowing you gave your all to the glory of God? Explain.

2. Striving so hard to please others in our relationships can keep us from being honest, open, and authentic. Pray for the courage to speak the truth in love, even when it would be easier to numbly go with the flow just to make everyone happy. Describe a time when you courageously spoke up or wish you had. Remember that He forgives you, even in those "I wish I would have" moments.

3. Read Acts 3–4 to grasp the bigger picture surrounding
the apostle Peter's bold proclamation of Christ. As you
do so, place your feet in Peter's sturdy sandals. Reflect on
his ability, by God's grace, to step before his disapprov-
ing adversaries and accusers. Have you faced a situation
in which you were challenged before others with opposing views?

4. What audiences watch your every move? As you serve
in your home, church, community, and beyond, how
can you be continually reminded that you live for an
audience of One? Check out Acts 17:28; Romans 14:8;
Galatians 2:20; and Philippians 1:21.

5. A woman I know once said, "I have worried way too
much about what people think when it matters only
what God thinks. And He thinks I'm pretty special!"
What does God think of you, His chosen and adopted
daughter in Christ? Make a Top Ten list and post it in
a prominent place where you will be reminded of your
value to God.

6. You have been with Jesus, filled with His grace and strengthened by His Word. You are changed and emboldened to step out in faith, even when doing so doesn't meet the approval of others. How do you seek God's approval instead? (Hint: Look back in the chapter for the answer; this is a trick question.)

7. What might your life on the edge look like as you step out—by the power of the Spirit—of an unhealthy need for the approval of others and into a life lived for an audience of One?

Write further
reflections here

CHAPTER SIX

Stepping Out of My Material Mind-set to a Life of Contentment

Baby Alive

I will never forget one of my favorite Christmas gifts as a child in the '70s. I wanted this gift in the worst way, and it all began with an ad in the Sears catalog, followed by a TV commercial: a little girl singing the jingle while cradling her baby doll: "I love the way you make me feel. You're so real." Baby Alive. As the advertising claim continued, "She's Baby Alive, and you can really feed her, give her a bottle, and change her diaper." Fascinating! What went in was sure to come out, and a child could thrill in both the feeding *and* the diapering aspects of parenting. She was the must-have girls' toy that Christmas. Today, that kind of toy craze turns mild-mannered shoppers into crazed monsters who fight over the last toy on the shelf. I don't know if any parents actually fought over Baby Alive, but I do know that the doll was in high demand.

I was sure I would feel pretty special, I was really some-body, if I could show off my very own doll, just like all the other little girls. I pleaded and begged. And on Christmas morning, my treasured Baby Alive was under the tree. Later that day, my cousin arrived, carrying her own brand-new doll that looked just like mine. We could hardly wait to fin-ish Christmas dinner, before running off to feed our babies. After mixing the powder that came with the doll with water to make her "food," we began to spoon the mixture into their moving mouths. Picture 1970s technology: mouths that moved robotically to the slow hum of the battery-pow-ered mechanisms inside.

Our babies were *hungry* that day. It was Christmas, af-ter all, so we kind of, umm, overfed them. We accidentally proved the advertising claim to be false, and we learned the sad truth that what goes in does not always come back out. (We used plenty of perfectly good D-batteries trying.) Before long, the mechanical operations died and my Baby Alive be-gan to smell funny. My must-have Christmas treasure was soon in the trash.

Maybe my Baby Alive incident sparked for you a simi-lar memory of a time when you wanted something in the worst way. But why begin this chapter with a silly story from my childhood when I could be confessing my *current* struggles with materialism? I did it because I think it is less embarrassing to admit that I obsessed about an object when I was too young to know better than it is to acknowledge a current materialistic mind-set.

But is it really? Fast-forwarding several years, there was a time when I just *had* to have countless pieces of knockoff designer-style clothing that promised popularity and fine fashion sense. Most of those clothes didn't last the season and were the next year's Goodwill donations. Then there was the time I *needed* the latest piece of aerobic exercise equipment because it guaranteed an ultra-fit figure. I used it a few times, and then it began gathering dust. Still later, I acquired a new sporty little car. It looked like a trophy sitting in the driveway, and I thought I would own it forever. We traded it off the very next year for a more practical family vehicle. Fast-forwarding again to present day, I open the desk drawer to find a stash of obsolete cell phones as I continue to trade up for the latest technology I can afford.

I wonder if I have learned anything about the here-today-and-gone-tomorrow qualities of the latest must-have treasures and trophies in this world.

Trophies

We could refer to many of our prized possessions as "trophies," couldn't we? That is kind of how we treat them. We keep our new furniture dusted and clean, threatening anyone who might approach our posh upholstery with a cup of red fruit juice or dirty shoes. We polish the chrome and coo over the SUV that graces the driveway the way we would fuss over a grand-prize medal. The home we're spending our life savings on sits as the jeweled crown of our accomplishments. None of these possessions, in and of themselves, are bad things, of course, but our attitude can cause the very things we own to end up owning us.

Do we cling too tightly to our things, measuring who we are by our prized possessions and by our accomplishments that enabled us to obtain them? Do we cherish them, claiming we are somebody by our stuff? There will come a time when all our most treasured possessions, all the cherished trophies of life, no longer grace our homes or our lives. Things break, wear out, or go out of style. Their significance will fade. They may be given away or discarded.

Jesus Steps In

I am reminded of the timeless hymn "The Old Rugged Cross." As I consider my trophies of this life now, the words of the chorus speak loud and clear to me:

> So I'll cherish the old rugged cross,
>   Till my trophies at last I lay down;
> I will cling to the old rugged cross,
>   And exchange it some day for a crown.

We cherish not trophies but Jesus Christ, who was slain for a world of lost sinners on a rough, rugged, and blood-stained cross. Because Jesus stepped in, bearing our pain and punishment as He took our sins upon Himself, we are redeemed. And because His redeeming power is at work in us today, we can lay down our trophies. As my beloved pastor emeritus once said, "You've got to have both hands free to cling to the cross!" Yes, by faith, we step out of our material mind-set, lay down the trophies, and cling only to the cross of the One in whom salvation is found. And we rejoice in the empty tomb! Jesus is risen, and we will one day receive the ultimate reward, the crown of glory, eternal life in Him—not because of any accomplishment of ours, but solely by His grace. And by the way, it feels pretty special knowing we are really somebody to our Savior, doesn't it? We each have the high honor of being His prized possession!

This brings me back, one more time, to my memory of a prized possession. Although Baby Alive didn't stick around very long, she provided a beautiful study in contrast that *has* stuck with me to this day:

- Another baby came to us some two thousand years ago, creating Christmas. He is with us still today.

- Jesus doesn't need to entice us with TV jingles or fancy advertisements to turn our hearts to Him; instead, He comes to us in His powerful Word and in the Sacraments.

- Jesus is not the latest craze that is here today and gone tomorrow, but He *does* make the news: He *is* the "good news of great joy . . . for all the people" (Luke 2:10), and His "steadfast love endures forever" (Psalm 100:5).

- We don't have to plead and beg, hoping to receive this treasured gift under the tree or anywhere else. It is ours by faith, anytime, anywhere.

- We love the way He makes us feel because He is real. He gives us real hope, real joy, real peace.

This baby, true God and true man, is God's perfect Son. This baby, who grew up to endure the agony of death on the cross on our behalf, also provided to us victory over eternal death. This baby is alive! And He lives in you today, by the power of the Holy Spirit. He gives you the greatest gift of all: eternal life, salvation in His name.

Treasures in Heaven

Jesus knew that the desire for and the distraction of worldly possessions were a danger to people. He knew the people of His day were easily enticed by wealth, just as we are today. He knows how readily we can let the love of money rule our hearts, so He addresses the subject powerfully in His Word.

We return, with crowds of Jesus' followers, to the mountainside on which He gave His famous sermon. Sit down among His followers in the crowd and listen to the wisdom of His words:

> Do not lay up for yourselves treasures on earth,
> where moth and rust destroy and where thieves
> break in and steal, but lay up for yourselves treasures
> in heaven, where neither moth nor rust
> destroys and where thieves do not break in and
> steal. For where your treasure is, there your
> heart will be also. . . . No one can serve two masters,
> for either he will hate the one and love the other,
> or he will be devoted to the one and despise the
> other. You cannot serve God and money.
> (Matthew 6:19–21, 24)

As Jesus spoke compassionately to the crowd, He did not say that we should own nothing in this world or deprive ourselves of any material possessions that may be of good use to us. After all, every good and perfect gift comes from His hand (James 1:17): home and food, clothing and transportation, income earned from an honest day's work. Even our gadgets, electronics, and labor-saving devices can be used for good and healthy purposes. Jesus was concerned, however, with our attitude toward earthly goods and our priority of them.

Where do our first priorities lie, and to what do we give our wholehearted attention? Do we give it to earthly treasure, the kind that is here today and gone tomorrow? The kind that moth and rust (and excessive quantities of Baby Alive food) can destroy? The kind that can be stolen from us?

Jesus reminds us, "Where your treasure is, there your heart will be also" (Matthew 6:21). When our hearts are wrapped around our prized possessions, we have a material mind-set. Our hearts and our minds dwell on whatever it is that we treasure most. If we wonder where our hearts lie, perhaps a good question to ask ourselves is how generous or stingy we are with our treasured earthly possessions. Would we willingly lay them down for the good of someone else?

Remember when I mentioned earlier how the things we own could end up owning us? This is exactly what Jesus means in verse 24: "You cannot serve God and money." (The Greek word here for *money* can mean either literal money or possessions.) We can so easily become a slave to our possessions, letting them control us. Christ is telling us to serve only God as our master, not our money and not our things.

Praise the Lord that He does not give up on us, even when our hearts are wrapped around our earthly treasures, even if we allow them to control us. By the work of the Holy Spirit in our hearts, He helps us make a priority shift so that instead, we can give our wholehearted attention to heavenly treasures. By God's grace in Christ, we have treasures such as faith, spiritual riches, forgiveness, and the promise of eternal life. These gifts are here today and still here tomorrow . . . and forever! They cannot be destroyed. And no one, not a thief, and not even the evil one, can break in and steal these eternal treasure from us. God's Holy Spirit helps us see how we can best use our earthly treasures for our good and for the good of others, all for His glory.

Reaffirming Christ's commands to us from His mountainside sermon are these words of the apostle Paul:

> As for the rich in this present age, charge them not to be haughty, nor to set their hopes on the uncertainty of riches, but on God, who richly provides us with everything to enjoy. They are to do good, to be rich in good works, to be generous and ready to share, thus storing up treasure for themselves as a good foundation for the future, so that they may take hold of that which is truly life. (1 Timothy 6:17–19)

Paul's play on the word *rich* has a special appeal to all of us. Compared with most of the present-day world, we *are* rich. We enjoy a roof over our heads, food on our table, and shoes on our feet . . . and so much more. We are rich, indeed. But we shouldn't be complacent in our wealth; we shouldn't rely on those earthly riches for our security—they could be snatched out from under us at any time. Instead, Paul tells us, we are to place our hope in God, who in His incomparable generosity richly provides every good thing that we need. God does this simply because He wants us to enjoy things. Therefore, in turn, we are to "be rich in good works," generous in sharing all that God has so generously given us. Our good works flow from us because of our faith in Christ, and He treasures them. He has taken hold of us, that we may take hold of the eternal treasure—life forever in Christ—that He freely gives to us.

A Stepping-Out Story

A few years ago, Katie accepted a position with a mission organization, packed her bags, and moved to Peru. For six years, she had prayed about doing mission work in Latin America, and one year after college graduation, with a year of experience teaching in a school with a strong Hispanic population, she was ready for this adventure.

While Katie had never been preoccupied with the latest trend or the newest technology, like many American young adults she was used to having many creature comforts, not the least of which included her laptop and her cell phone. She knew, as she prepared to move to Peru, that she would be stepping out of the American material-minded culture (quite literally!) into a culture that did not enjoy all the same luxuries. Still, she was grateful for the opportunity to take her laptop so she could communicate with her family back home and to post updates to her blog for all who supported her mission work.

In the mission field, Katie taught English as an inroad to establish relationships and to share the Gospel. She reached out to the people of Peru by leading Bible studies, children's ministries, and more. Her time there was unforgettable.

Nearly two years later, when her assignment came to a close and she returned home, she was caught off guard by how many changes had taken place in the United States, especially in the area of electronic technology. She had not realized how much she, too, had changed until she embarked on an adventure with her father to buy a new cell phone.

Prior to her time in Peru, Katie owned a basic track phone with no data plan and no special features. And she had been content with that. Upon her return, she was overwhelmed by the advances in cell-phone technology and by how many sophisticated devices her peers had acquired: tablets, smart phones, and such.

She knew she needed a way to communicate, because she would be traveling extensively throughout the U.S. to share the story of her missionary journey. So three days after her return, she went with her father to the cell phone store. But the minute she walked through the door, she experienced a panicky deer-in-headlights moment; she couldn't even look at a specific phone. "Dad, I can't do this," she whispered, and they left.

Knowing she needed to get over this hurdle, they tried another store. This time, she brought herself to actually look at the assortment of phones available to her, but she was shocked by the prices. Her mind reeled as she considered the people she had recently worked with in Latin America. The price of one phone could pay for food for an entire family for weeks. Still, she consoled herself, it would just be a one-time cost. Then the store representative began rattling off the additional cost of service plans. Tears welled in Katie's eyes as she heard all sorts of options she didn't even understand, all for a hefty monthly fee. "Dad, I can't do this right now." She ran out of the store in tears, too stressed to make a decision.

After a third trip and still no phone, Katie came to a conclusion she shared with her father, "I am not spending that much money on a cell phone right now. God blessed me with those experiences abroad and the relationships with the people I worked with for two years. I know that they are struggling to put food on the table, and I just can't do this now."

Katie's dad had a great solution. He handed back to her the simple phone she had used before her two years overseas. He knew what was best for his daughter at this difficult time of transition.

Katie had been forewarned by other missionaries to expect a change of heart upon returning to the States, especially concerning possessions. But she didn't expect the change to shock her so much. Since her return, the material mindset has disgusted her. She easily recognizes how marketing ads and campaigns target feelings and attempt to make people feel disconnected and inferior if they don't have the latest gadgets.

Still content with simplicity, Katie continues her studies in education. She knows she will need to learn to use the latest technology to be an effective teacher. She is trying to come to grips with the necessary expenses for such. "When I even think about spending money on something beyond the basics, I feel the people from Peru on my heart. It's convicting."

While it may seem that Katie is hesitant to embrace technology, she sees great value in it, realizing it can provide new methods for outreach and more means of reaching people and helping them connect with Christ. At the same time, she thinks about the story of her cell phone and hopes that everyone would wrestle with such a decision and pray before committing to large purchases and monthly fees. She suggests people ask themselves: Why do I need this? How can it benefit another? How else could this money be used?

"The longer I am back," she confesses, "the easier it is to justify purchases based on what others around me have." The Lord continues to use Katie's mission experience to draw her to a life on the edge, away from a material mindset to which she could so easily be drawn. A favorite verse serves as a powerful reminder: "Do not be conformed to this world, but be transformed by the renewal of your mind, that by testing you may discern what is the will of God, what is good and acceptable and perfect" (Romans 12:2). Katie knows that the Lord has used her time in the mission field as an experience in which the Holy Spirit speaks very clearly to her about the difference between what she needs and what she wants. "And," she adds with a smile, "you don't have to go to Peru to learn this."

Life on the Edge = the Abundant Life

In John 10:10, Jesus says, "I came that [you] may have life and have it abundantly." He gives us life eternal, now and forever, by His sacrificial death and resurrection for our sins. He fills our lives with blessings beyond measure, enabling us to live a truly abundant life—a life on the edge with Christ.

But sometimes even well-meaning Christians misinterpret Christ's message of the abundant life to mean financial or physical prosperity in the here and now. Misguided messengers may claim that God wants us to have it all now! This is the world's voice, not God's.

The world screams, "More!" More money. More status. More stuff. More entertainment. More everything. So we chase after one more thing, thinking it will surely provide the abundant life, only to find that there is always one more thing after that and that not only are we *not* overflowing with blessed abundance, but we feel depleted at every turn by abundant stress and perhaps abundant debt. Meanwhile, our focus is taken off of what it means to have real abundant life.

The abundant life of which Jesus speaks is the life of spiritual abundance, a life filled with contentment and gratitude in every situation; in the midst of, or despite, our circumstances. "In any and every circumstance, I have learned the secret of facing plenty and hunger, abundance and need. I can do all things through him who strengthens me" (Philippians 4:12–13). Christ is the source of and the secret to our contentment in all circumstances.

I must admit that left to myself, I would still cower behind that same old diving board. I would stand with my hoarded piles of treasured possessions and the stuff that I was certain would provide the abundant life. But I am not left to myself. Thanks to Jesus' heart-changing work in me, I don't cower there any longer. In Jesus' firm grip, I step out from behind the board and follow Him to the edge.

- Living on the edge, I can be content and grateful for all that I have and even for what I don't have. I can trust that God, in His wisdom, may lovingly spare me from some earthly treasure I think I want. He does all of this for my greater good. Whatever my circumstances, whether I live by meager means or by bountiful boatloads (according to the world's definition of abundance), He fills me with His fullness so that I would seek first the things of God, laying up treasures in heaven.

- Living on the edge, I can trust in God's great provision for all my material and spiritual needs. "And my God will supply every need of yours according to His riches in glory in Christ Jesus" (Philippians 4:19). He gives abundantly and provides you and me with every necessary thing—and so much more.

- Living on the edge, I know that He will never leave me; that He is completely dependable. I can count on Him to always be with me, filling me with contentment and leading me to recognize that everything I have is a gift from His hand. "Keep your life free from love of money, and be content with what you have, for He has said, 'I will never leave you nor forsake you'" (Hebrews 13:5).

Reflections

1. What gift have you wanted in the worst way?
   Did your treasure eventually turn to trash?

2. Have you clung tightly to things, measuring who
   you are by your prized possessions or your accomplishments that enabled you to obtain such things? Explain.
   (Remember: You are really somebody to your Savior;
   you are His prized possession.)

3. Recall these words from page 119: "Jesus is not the
   latest craze that is here today and gone tomorrow, but
   He does make the news: He *is* the 'good news.'" Check
   out just a sampling of this Good News: Luke 2:10–11;
   John 3:16; Acts 4:10–12; Romans 3:22–24; Romans 6:23;
   1 Corinthians 15:3–4. Reflect on these passages.

4. Read Matthew 6:19–24, a powerful portion of the Sermon on the Mount. As you do, slip your feet into the sandals of one of Christ's followers who was there that day, sitting down to listen. Are you convicted as you hear His words and consider the earthly treasures you have wrapped your heart around? Then overjoyed as you hear that His heavenly treasure for you cannot be destroyed or taken away? Share further thoughts.

5. Name some of the heavenly treasures we have by God's grace in Christ—the kind that last forever.

6. Do you consider yourself rich? rich in good works? richly provided for by God? How might you be able to use your earthly treasures, by His grace, to benefit others and bring glory to God?

7. In what ways may you fall for the lies of the world that tell you more will make you happy?
   What is real abundant life?

8. What might your life on the edge look like,
   as you step out of your material mind-set to a place
   of contentment, where Christ would have you live?

Write further
reflections here:

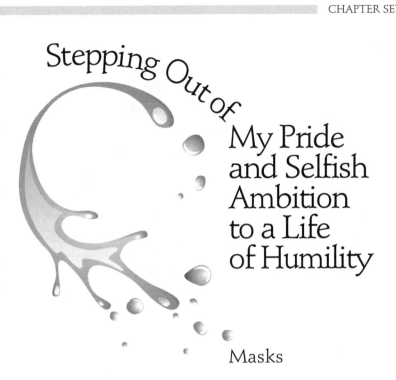

CHAPTER SEVEN

Stepping Out of My Pride and Selfish Ambition to a Life of Humility

Masks

I have a secret stash of masks that I keep handy for all those times when, for a variety of reasons that you will soon know, I am feeling particularly prideful. My assortment of masks does a nice job of concealing the truth that lies beneath them. So I slap them on as needed.

When life decisions, large or small, need to be made, pride would have me say, "It's my decision. It's my life. I'll live it however I want to." That's when I slap on my In–Charge Mask. Sporting this mask, I try to convince myself and others that I can take the driver's seat, make all my own decisions, and operate under my own power regarding everything from relationships to finances, from my career plans to my moral and ethical choices. Oh, and by the way, when I am wearing this mask, pride has me believe that I am never wrong. After all, a go-to gal like me, in charge of her own life, could never make a mistake. Right?

On other occasions, when a loved one or a trusted friend asks, "How have you been, Deb?", instead of revealing the truth (which might sound something like, "I've been struggling lately"), I slap on my I'm-Fine Mask. You know, the one that gives the impression that everything is just great. "Couldn't be better." Why? The difficult truth stares me in the face (under that mask, of course): Pride. Again. Oh, sure, I can justify my answer: "Oh, I don't want to bother them. They have enough worries of their own." The truth is, though, that I don't want them to see me in my weakness. Yep, that is a pride issue. To admit that I am struggling with something—anything—is to admit weakness, dependency on others, or the need for help. And I don't need help. Right? I can do it all on my own.

In similar situations, I want to have all the answers—at church, at school, at home. As an example, when attending a Bible study, I want to give the right answers, should someone ask. So I slap on the Answer Mask, the one that lets everyone think that I am super knowledgeable, that they need only look to me for a quick answer. Ouch. Does pride keep me from learning from and listening to others? And does it inhibit others from answering or sharing? Could it even keep me from attending Bible study or another learning opportunity because I don't want to reveal my lack of understanding or inability to answer? Maybe.

What mask should I wear for those times when I drive by another car and think proudly, "Look at that old jalopy; mine is nicer than theirs"? Or when I stare at someone's lack of fashion sense or poor hygiene, their addictive habits or embarrassing behaviors, and say smugly under my breath, "Well, at least I'm not *that* bad"? For these proud moments, there is the ever-popular Better-Than-You Mask. Because I *am* just a bit better. Aren't I?

Every mask attempts to conceal some important truths—and they are more than a bit humbling:

- I am *not* in charge of my own life, and I do make mistakes.

- I am weak, and I could use some help.

- I don't have all the answers.

- I am no better than the next person.

Jesus Steps In

The truth is that God is the Lord of our lives, and we are not. In our sinful pride, we fail to follow His leading. We put our trust in ourselves instead of in Him. We think we know better than He does. On our own, we are stuck in our selfish sins. It is only by the work of the Holy Spirit in our hearts that we can confess our sins of pride and ask Him to show us where and when we are too full of ourselves. With repentant hearts, we surrender our pride, yield our lives to His lordship, and humble ourselves before our God. In His limitless mercy, He washes us clean in Christ, covering these countless sins with His pure and perfect forgiveness. Because Jesus steps in, it is possible for us to step out of our pride, to lay aside the masks that caused us to try to conceal the truth from ourselves.

Humility begins as He enables me to recognize my proper place in relation to my Maker. No longer do I trust in my ways and my desires, but in His. Humility does not selfishly ask, "What do I want to do today?" but "Lord, what would You have me do today?" and then seeks His Word and follows His lead. Humility is putting God in His proper place as Lord of my life, and me in my proper place at His feet. Good-bye, In-Charge Mask! "For My thoughts are not your thoughts, neither are your ways My ways, declares the LORD. For as the heavens are higher than the earth, so are My ways higher than your ways and My thoughts than your thoughts" (Isaiah 55:8–9).

As the Lord enables me to recognize my helplessness and accept my weaknesses, I learn reliance on His power and on others' help. It is humbly freeing to admit to another Christian, "I am struggling and would like your prayers." Farewell, I'm-Fine Mask! "But He said to me, 'My grace is sufficient for you, for My power is made perfect in weakness.' Therefore I will boast all the more gladly of my weaknesses, so that the power of Christ may rest upon me" (2 Corinthians 12:9).

My Savior helps me to accept a position of humility, where I listen and learn from others. He gives me an appropriate perspective in which I can say things such as, "I don't have it all together, but I trust the One who does." And, "I don't know the answer to that, but I will try to find out from someone who does know, and then I will get back to you." Adios, Answer Mask! "To make an apt answer is a joy to a man, and a word in season, how good it is!" (Proverbs 15:23).

God gives me eyes to see His other children as He sees them: loved and valuable and—just like me—in need of a Savior. He enables me to stop judging them in my pride and start loving them by His grace. Bye, bye, Better-Than-You Mask! "For by the grace given to me I say to everyone among you not to think of himself more highly than he ought to think, but to think with sober judgment, each according to the measure of faith that God has assigned" (Romans 12:3).

A friend shared with me how God is working in her life in regard to pride: "When I fail, I need to be transparent enough to admit my failure instead of trying to put on a prideful act to make me look better to others. When I succeed, I am reminded that the success comes from God, and I humbly give Him the credit." "Clothe yourselves, all of you, with humility toward one another, for 'God opposes the proud but gives grace to the humble'" (1 Peter 5:5).

Make no mistake, the only reason we can lay aside our masks of pride and clothe ourselves with humility is because Jesus has stepped into our lives with His grace and forgiveness, filling us with faith. Jesus showed us the greatest extent of humility with His very life, as shared poetically in the Spirit-inspired words of the apostle Paul:

> Have this mind among yourselves, which is yours
> in Christ Jesus, who, though he was in the form of
> God, did not count equality with God a thing to be

grasped, but emptied Himself, by taking the form of a servant, being born in the likeness of men. And being found in human form, He humbled Himself by becoming obedient to the point of death, even death on a cross. Therefore God has highly exalted Him and bestowed on Him the name that is above every name, so that at the name of Jesus every knee should bow, in heaven and on earth and under the earth, and every tongue confess that Jesus Christ is Lord, to the glory of God the Father. (Philippians 2:5–11)

This passage begins with the words "have this mind." What is *this mind?* It is one of humility. The message of true humility is unique to Christians. This isn't to say that people of other world religions are incapable of being humble. No, but true humility was exemplified and personified only in Christ. No other religion teaches this. Other world religions take a prideful position, claiming that men can become gods, seek power, or achieve salvation by their own good works. Only in the Christian faith do we find the unthinkable, the opposite: God humbled Himself and became man. Why? Because of His great love for us!

Jesus left His Father and heaven to come to earth with the single-focused mission of saving us from our sin, separated us from God. And He did this through the humblest of all circumstances. He entered the womb of a peasant girl and came to the world in meekness, a helpless but perfect infant, fully man yet fully God in the flesh. He lived a perfect life in this sin-filled world, died a most cruel and humiliating death, and rose from the dead, conquering sin and the grave, that we prideful, selfish sinners might be forgiven. Exalted by the Father, Jesus is the One whose name we confess as Lord and Savior, to the glory of God! He is our hope of salvation.

A Selfish Request

As Jesus steps into our lives with a message of true humility that opposes the prideful and selfish ways of the world, so He also stepped into the lives of His followers with messages that continuously rocked their world.

In Mark 10:35–45, two of Jesus' closest comrades approached Him with a prideful and selfish request. James and John had clearly been communicating between themselves, formulating a plan with which to approach Jesus. They said, "Teacher, we want You to do for us whatever we ask of You" (v. 35). *Whoa!* They hadn't even asked their question yet, and they wanted Jesus to grant it to them. Gutsy. Jesus was patient with them. He knew where this was going, of course, as He asked what they wanted Him to do for them.

Then they made their bold request, "Grant us to sit, one at Your right hand and one at Your left, in Your glory" (v. 37). Definitely a bold request, and it was not one they would have discussed first with the other disciples. I imagine that James and John probably tiptoed over to Jesus, hoping that no one else would hear. They wanted to make sure they got the best seats in the house, the loftiest positions next to the King. But they were confused (as the disciples often were); they were short sighted about Jesus' mission and His kingdom. They envisioned Christ on the glorious throne of an earthly kingdom, and they desired to hold the first and second positions of power next to Him. Pride and selfish ambition were written all over their request.

Jesus gently rebuked them, telling them they did not know what they were really asking. To be in Christ's kingdom would not mean an earthly throne of gold or a position of power—it would mean trouble, hardship, and persecution. Jesus asked if they would be willing or able to suffer alongside Him and endure the rough road that lay ahead. Naively, James and John nodded their heads, claiming they were, indeed, willing.

Jesus then foretold that they would endure great suffering as His followers, all for the sake of the Gospel. Jesus' answer was not exactly what they hoped for or expected. But before we pick on James and John too much for their bold appeal to Jesus, we should take a look at the responses of the others. When the news of the brothers' request reached the other ten disciples, they were more than a little miffed with James and John. Perhaps they mumbled, "How dare those two make such a request, asking for the number one and two spots next to the throne!" Perhaps pride was rearing its ugly head among these disciples too, and along with it, a hearty serving of selfish ambition. Why did the request bother them so much? Perhaps because they, too, desired to sit next to the throne in the places of highest honor. Each wanted to be in the number-one seat because each was merely looking out for number one.

So Jesus called all of the disciples together and attempted to set things straight: "You know that those who are considered rulers of the Gentiles lord it over them, and their great ones exercise authority over them. But it shall not be so among you. But whoever would be great among you must be your servant, and whoever would be first among you must be slave of all" (vv. 42–44). The disciples were well aware of the Gentile rulers' oppressive reign. Those who were considered great in the Roman world were the rulers and authorities. Jesus was turning the disciples' world on its ear by telling them that His kingdom would be quite different. In fact, it would be just the opposite. Those in authority would serve those beneath them. Those who would be great in God's kingdom would be servants to all.

Jesus continued, "For even the Son of Man came not to be served but to serve, and to give His life as a ransom for many" (v. 45). Jesus, Lord of all, the One with highest authority, could have demanded that He be served. He had every right to. But instead, He placed the disciples' needs and our needs ahead of His own in humble servant leadership. He went further still, so far as to give His life in exchange for their pardon and ours. His was the ultimate act of humble service and sacrifice.

Humble Service

Only hours before Jesus went to the cross, He showed His disciples what He meant by serving instead of being served. He gave them, and us, a beautiful, lasting impression of what it means to place others' needs ahead of our own.

What did He do? In the Upper Room during the Passover meal, just before His betrayal and arrest, Jesus got up from the meal they shared and began washing His disciples' feet.

Understand that in the time and culture, this was a degrading job, held by the lowest servant of the household.

Jesus was their Master, yet He performed the lowliest and humblest of duties. In a selfless act of love and service, He washed their dirty, stinky feet. And He took it a step further: He told them that they were to go and do the same for one another. Jesus said, "If I then, your Lord and Teacher, have washed your feet, you also ought to wash one another's feet. For I have given you an example, that you also should do just as I have done to you" (John 13:14–15). If they were to lead, they first needed to serve. They were to be willing to do the dirty work, for His sake. The disciples would be the first Christian leaders teaching the faith. What Jesus set for them was the perfect example of what a humble servant-leader does.

When we lead, we are to follow this model. We are to lead by serving others in humility, living lives of sacrifice for their good. In all our relationships, we are to place the needs of others ahead of our own by getting down on our knees and doing the dirty work. The apostle Paul exhorts us: "Do nothing from selfish ambition or conceit, but in humility count others more significant than yourselves. Let each of you look not only to his own interests, but also to the interests of others" (Philippians 2:3–4). It is not wrong for us to have our own interests and to tend to our own needs as long as we keep them in check, placing them in the right perspective in relation to the Lord and to others, whom we serve.

The Energy Gauge

Several years ago, when asked to help with a household chore, my clever six-year-old slumped his shoulders and replied, "But, Mom, my energy gauge is practically on empty."

My quizzical expression prompted him to continue: "You see, Mom, normally my gauge is like this," and he stretched his arms wide. "But right now, it's almost gone, like this," and he held his thumb and forefinger a quarter of an inch apart. His gauge was curiously full a few minutes earlier when he was at play, doing exactly as he pleased. Now, when asked to complete a chore, it was dangerously low. Mind you, the chore was not something dreadful; it was merely assisting me with the meal, something he usually loved to do.

I chuckled as I went on with my task, but I wondered if my little guy was inadvertently teaching me a thing or two about my own desire to do exactly as I pleased and give in to my susceptibility toward selfish ambition. Does his energy gauge resonate with you too?

We invest our energies in all sorts of areas, don't we? We put so much energy into *our* daily work: career, hobbies, recreation, and even household chores (our to-do lists, if you will), that we may find our energy gauge practically on empty when it's time to help someone else or when it's time for devotion with the Lord.

Have we pretended not to notice when our neighbor is in need, because we are just too preoccupied with our own interests to take the time for someone else? Do we go through the motions as we worship, because our mind is on other priorities? Might we complain that we just don't have energy left when a friend asks us to pray for her? Are our tanks dangerously low when the church needs volunteers to teach and serve? And what about when we sit down for a few minutes of devotion time with our Savior? Sometimes, our energy gauges read empty before we've given any of our energy to the Lord and to His Word.

Even as we listen to a friend or participate in conversation with a group, do we attempt to turn the topic back to ourselves, perhaps without even realizing it, all because we are bursting with selfish energy? As another person talks, sometimes I can't wait for her to finish so I can interject with my brilliant example for her from *my* life or my obvious solution to her problem, based on my experience or vast wisdom (cue eye rolling here).

Just as the disciples' selfish request of Jesus revealed their desire to look out for number one, we, too, have selfish ambition. Praise God for His continual refueling process through His forgiveness in Christ. Through the Holy Spirit, He gives us faith to trust Him for a fresh start each day, with a gauge reading full and the power and desire to serve Him and His people in all the ways His energy directs us, placing their needs ahead of our own.

A Stepping-Out Story

Six years into marriage, my husband, Cory, and I were living in Frisco, Texas, and life was good. We were blessed with a healthy marriage and two terrific toddlers, and we had purchased our first home. We were active in a growing church. Cory was enjoying a fulfilling corporate career, and I was loving life as a stay-at-home mom with the twins. Despite all this, there was unrest in our home. We wanted to move to the Great Plains, back home, to be closer to extended family. I especially did. My prideful, selfish heart was *so* certain of what it wanted.

So I began to push Cory, who in turn began to push his boss. Cory asked if the company could help him transfer to the Midwest or the Great Plains (specifically, South Dakota), where he would still be able to keep his position within the company. Believe it or not, it looked like there was a way. Oddly enough, a single position was posted for a little town in South Dakota. Now, keep in mind, there aren't many openings in that rural state for *any* kind of corporate position, so this looked like the chance of a lifetime. We assumed that it must be a "God thing."

Cory's boss inquired. And we waited. And we waited. I became so impatient that it was all I could think about. I would sit by the phone daily, waiting for Cory's call, anticipating that *this* would be the day he would hear something! Nothing. I prodded him and nudged him to keep nudging his boss. I cried out to the Lord. Surely *He* would want us to live closer to our parents and families.

It was my selfish ambition to make sure this move happened. I even went so far as to tell Cory over the phone one day, "You know, God helps those who help themselves." What I was really saying was, "Get on it, Buddy! God will help us make this happen if we just make the first move and force it along a little!"

The job opportunity never happened. God closed that door. Actually, I don't think He ever really opened it in the first place. As it turned out, the job was posted as a formality only; the company never intended to fill it. So much for *our* plans. How humbling.

"But, Deb, how about Des Moines, Iowa?" Cory asked.

We had lived there briefly when we were first married. "If we really want to get back to the Midwest, I could call my old boss."

Yuck. I had no desire to return to Des Moines. When we lived there for the first few months of our marriage, we resided in a rough neighborhood with the worst possible next-door neighbors. (Remember the townhouse in one of my opening stories?) No way! Once again, my prideful heart thought it knew best. I did *not* want to move to Des Moines, Iowa.

Meanwhile, another possibility came our way. Cory's company opened an account in Fargo, North Dakota, and he was sent there to train employees. While visiting, we even consulted a Realtor. But it was not to be. *Slam!* went another door. Cory attempted to console me with the words "There is always Iowa, Deb!"

Ugh. "Well . . . okay. I guess. Go ahead and look into it." (Cue heavy sigh here.) *What will it hurt?* I thought. *This lead will come to nothing, just like the others.*

Cory talked to his former boss, who said there would be a position waiting for him—no interview required. He could start work as soon as we could arrive. *What?!* I had been humbled not just once, but twice. What was God planning to do now? Send us somewhere I didn't want to go?

I was six months pregnant, and we had a house to sell. It didn't look to me like the perfect timing for a job transfer, but the Lord kept opening doors wide. Our house sold in one week, and we moved in my seventh month of pregnancy.

Only by the grace of God was I able to swallow my pride

and walk through this wide-open door. We humbly believed and admitted that the Lord knew best. We even chuckled that we had better follow where He was clearly leading us, because He had been very direct about shutting doors to places we thought we wanted to go to

Our move to Des Moines was a tremendous blessing for me and for our entire family. The years that followed were years of great faith growth, filled with God's provision of a church home and people He used to help Cory recognize His call to full-time ministry. I meekly admit now that the very place I thought I would despise came to be one of my favorites.

In my selfish desire to take charge of my life, I thought I knew best, and I expected the Lord to come alongside my plans. My pride could have kept us from going to the place where He had tremendous blessings in store for us. That year, I feasted on heaping helpings of humble pie as my Savior taught me a lot about pride and humility. In the process, He also taught me about His grace. Although I kept stubbornly going my own selfish way, He did not give up on me, but gently persisted in His perfect plans for me and my family, forgiving me and healing me of my sinful pride as He patiently worked on my heart and in my life.

Remember that gross misstatement I made to my husband concerning God's help? The opposite is closer to the truth. You see, the Lord helps those who *cannot* help themselves. Prideful, selfish sinners like you and me. We are helpless to save ourselves from this pathetic place in which we find ourselves trapped in our sin. But the Lord helps the helpless: For by grace you have been saved through faith. And this is not your own doing; it is the gift of God, not a result of works, so that no one may boast. (Ephesians 2:8–9)

Life on the Edge

I am back to my diving board, still very thankful that it's not a real one, and wondering how I am going to get from this prideful, selfish place behind the board and out there to the edge, where Christ would have me live. It's as if a tall stack of floatie rings is piled up on the cement in front of me. My tall stack of arrogant pride and selfish ambition is piled so high and standing in my way that I can't even see the edge. I am unable to move them out of the way. Then my Savior comes to the rescue and removes the towering stack from my path. He leads me to confess my sins and enables me to see clearly from a new and humble perspective. He leads me to a life on the edge.

Here are a few prayers that I pray along the way, as Jesus enables me to step out of my pride and selfish ambition and moves me to a life of humility on the edge:

- I pray that I would look only to Him as Lord of my life. "What would *You* have me do today, Lord?"

- I pray for the strength to admit my weaknesses and my inability to have all the answers.

- I pray for humility in my relationships so that I would ask others what they need, serve without expecting anything in return, and listen more than I speak in my conversations with them.

- I pray that I would humbly admit my failures
  and give God the glory in every success.

Living on the edge, by His amazing grace, I surrender my pride as I acknowledge who God is and praise Him for His mighty Spirit at work in me. He who stretched the heavens and made the earth, the incredible creation all around me, is my almighty, all-powerful Creator (Isaiah 51:13). His love is so vast and so great that He sent a Savior to die for me, even as I was in the midst of my sin (Romans 5:8). No one can begin to fathom the mysteries of God because His wisdom and knowledge are beyond human comprehension (Romans 11:33). Even the difficult circumstances He allows in my life have a purpose far greater than I can begin to understand (Romans 8:28). All circumstances are for His glory and my good, and He may allow them for the purpose of growing my faith and trust in Him (James 1:2–4).

I consider the position in which I pray. Why do I bow my head or get on my knees? It's all about humility, admitting my smallness next to His greatness and yielding my will to my Creator's will in prayer and in life. "Oh come, let us worship and bow down; let us kneel before the LORD, our Maker!" (Psalm 95:6).

Reflections

1. Which mask of pride do you find yourself slapping on most often these days? The In-Charge Mask, the I'm-Fine Mask, the Answer Mask, or the Better-Than-You Mask? Maybe you have another mask of pride you wear, concealing the truth that lies behind it. Prompted by the Spirit, confess your sins to the One who freely forgives. Pray for Christ's strength to lay aside each mask and live a life of humility.

2. Read Mark 10:35–45. As you do, place your feet into James's and John's selfish sandals as they approached Jesus with their bold request. How did Jesus' answers rock their world? After Christ foretold that they, too, would suffer for the sake of the Gospel, how well do you think they comprehended His humbling words?

3. Have you ever made a prideful, selfish request, only to find that it was inappropriate or misguided? How were you humbled?

4. Ponder the extent of the Father's love for you, that He would send His Son to die in exchange for your pardon. Sing the words of Philippians 2:6–11, an early hymn of praise of Christ's humility and exaltation, to the glory of God! Make up your own tune or sing the words to the tune of a familiar hymn or song; whether you sing on- or off-key, you will be making a joyful noise to the Lord! (Check out Psalm 98 for more about making a joyful noise.)

5. Read John 13:1–17, the account of Jesus washing the disciples' feet on the night of His betrayal and arrest. His was an enormous gesture of humble service and love and an example for us to follow. How can you, prompted by the Spirit, serve others today? What lowly tasks might you be asked to perform in service to others?

6. We all have something similar to an energy gauge. How do you use your time and energy? Primarily in the pursuit of selfish ambitions? Or in the interest of serving others first? How can you make sure you have plenty of energy for a daily devotion and prayer? Ask for energy from the Lord and the strength to step out to serve.

7. What might your life on the edge look like, as you step out of your pride and selfish ambition by the power of the Spirit to a place of humility, where Christ would have you live?

Write further reflections here

CHAPTER EIGHT

Stepping Out of My Judgmental Attitude to a Life of Grace

The Label Maker

I have this great label maker. It is reminiscent of the vintage 1970s model that I had as a child—the kind where you turn the dial to the correct letter, then squeeze the handle really hard, and presto, an impression is made on a little roll of sticky-backed thick plastic tape. After spelling an entire word or phrase, several clicks of the handle would send the imprinted tape out of the machine with the letters pressed firmly into it, ready to cut, peel, and adhere to the next label-worthy item. I could press and print any word I wanted, label anything or anyone. Yes, my '70s-model label maker made labeling a cinch. "DEBBIE KAY HUDSON" was spelled across the back of my child-size motorcycle helmet. "MY JEWELRY" or "SAFETY PINS & SUCH" were stuck to special containers. "PRETTY" or "STUPID" may have been slapped on my sister, depending on my sassiness or mood at the moment.

The label maker I carry today is not limited to the technology of the time. This current model is quite different and very versatile. Today, I create labels in my mind, not so much for things anymore, but most certainly for people. And this label maker operates with ease. This is how it works: I meet someone or see her on the street. Maybe I know her already. Regardless, I take one look or listen to her for a moment, and quickly form an opinion, good or bad. (Ah, but the bad opinions form the fastest.)

My dial begins to turn. Click. Click. Click. Before long, I have impressed a word or a phrase firmly in my mind. And, presto, the label appears before me: BAD MOM. ALCOHOLIC. COWARD. CLUELESS. TOO PRETTY. SELFISH. UNREACHABLE. TOO DIFFERENT FROM ME. SINNER. Just like that. I mentally adhere it to the person I feel is label-worthy. (If I thought label-making in the '70s was a cinch, this is even easier!) It is easy to slap a label on someone and then walk away. Labeling provides an excuse to exclude, a defense to avoid discussion, a reason to justify my judgment toward this woman or that man who is also a child of God. Ouch. Hmm. Also a child of God, you say?

I'm embarrassed to admit this, but often my initial reaction to the people around me is to put them in a category. Using my "A" list, I judge by **Appearance** before I get to know them: "She is dressed too sloppily to have a decent job." I judge by **Assumption**, based on little to no evidence: "Well, I just assumed she wasn't a Christian by the way she talked." I judge by **Association**, based on the reputation of family or friend (often called "guilt by association"): "He must be up to no good; after all, look what his brothers did."

I wonder how Jesus responds when He looks at these same people. Actually, I already know the answer to that. During His earthly ministry, when Jesus met people on the street, He didn't make assumptions. He already knew everything about them: their faults and their failures, their sins and their shortcomings. He took more than one look at them, and it was not to judge their appearance but to have compassion on them. Jesus was not afraid to be associated with the socially unacceptable. Were He to have placed a label on them, it would have been only to completely cover all the hurtful, judgmental labels the world had slapped on them. Jesus would choose labels like these: FORGIVEN. REDEEMED. LOVED BY GOD. HEALED BY CHRIST. CHILD OF GOD. MADE BEAUTIFUL IN JESUS.

Christ did not exclude the people on the fringes of society, the sinners, or the outcasts. Instead, He went out of His way to bring hope, forgiveness, and healing to them. He did not avoid discussions with others. Instead, He seized every opportunity to share the truth in love and teach about the kingdom of God. Although He alone, by His divine authority, would have been justified in judging and condemning sinners, He chose instead to pardon them and set them free.

Go, and Sin No More

On one such occasion during His ministry, Jesus had come to the temple to teach, and great crowds gathered around Him to listen and to learn from Him (John 8:1–11). As Jesus sat in the middle of the people teaching them, the scribes and Pharisees burst onto the scene, dragging a woman with them and making a public spectacle of her, forcing her to stand in the center of the crowd. Sobbing, she had been shamed. Trapped, caught, and labeled by those who had found her naked and guilty of the sin of adultery. Adulteress. Sinner. Worthy of death. With the intent to set a snare for Jesus, hoping to find something with which to condemn Him as well, the scribes and Pharisees exclaimed, "Teacher, this woman has been caught in the act of adultery. Now in the Law Moses commanded us to stone such women. So what do You say?" (vv. 4–5). (Actually, they had it only partially right. The Law, according to Leviticus 20:10 and Deuteronomy 22:22, said that both the man and the woman caught in the act of adultery should be stoned. Where was the man? Had they singled out the woman, letting the man go free, entrapping only her that she may be used as an example before Jesus in order to also entrap Him?)

As you envision this scene, you can almost see the sneers on their faces and their beady little eyes narrowed in His direction, looking for an answer they could use to bring a charge against Him.

Jesus bent down and wrote with His finger on the ground. And as they continued to ask Him, He stood and said, "Let him who is without sin among you be the first to throw a stone at her." And once more He bent down and wrote on the ground (vv. 6–8).

Jesus did not avoid this difficult discussion. Instead, He boldly confronted the legalism of the Jewish leaders and used it to bring their own judgment right back upon them. Jesus did not allow the scribes and Pharisees to justify their judgment against the woman with a terse quote of the Law. They attempted not only to slap a label on the woman, but also to convict her and stone her. But even they, for all their legalistic entrapments of others, could not pretend to be without sin. They couldn't stone her, because they were guilty too. So they slithered away, one by one. Can you hear the stones that slipped from their hands and hit the ground as they went?

Jesus stepped in that day, disqualifying the Jewish leaders from their judgmental position. I would love to be able to tell you that in response, they stepped out of their hypercritical attitude. But although they walked away from this judgment call, their hearts were hardened, and they refused to learn from Jesus. Instead, they looked all the more for ways to ensnare Him. However, we can believe that there were others in the crowd who took Jesus' message of grace to heart that day, stepping out of their own judgmental, critical attitude toward others.

> Jesus was left alone with the woman standing before Him. Jesus stood up and said to her, "Woman, where are they? Has no one condemned you?" She said, "No one, Lord." And Jesus said, "Neither do I condemn you; go, and from now on sin no more." (vv. 9–11)

Jesus knew her guilt, her sin, her shame. He didn't excuse any of it away. Instead, He called her to repent of it, to live a new life forgiven of the guilt and shame of her sin. Jesus covered the woman's labels with His forgiveness. What did

He write in the sand that day? No one is sure. Because the Jewish leaders were expecting Jesus to act as judge over this woman, He may have been writing His sentence before pronouncing it, as judges often did at that time.

But perhaps Jesus was writing a beautiful new label of grace. One that pronounced freedom, as He proclaimed to the woman, "Go, and . . . sin no more." By the Law, her sin was deserving of a death sentence, but by God's grace in Christ, she was no longer condemned. By the Gospel, she was forgiven and set free to step out of her sinful life into a new life of repentance. She could leave her old life behind, all because Jesus stepped in to her world and set her free. Imagine her first breath of freedom as she walked down the road that day. Jesus enabled her to break free from who and what she was and embrace her new identity in Christ. The only labels she bore now were the ones He mercifully gave her: SAVED. FORGIVEN. FREE.

Jesus Steps In

God alone knows the heart of each person; only He is able to rightly judge. Satan points his accusing finger in our direction, and often, so does the world. They slap all sorts of hurtful labels on us, charging us with sins worthy of a death sentence. And the truth is we recognize most of those labels. Not just because we have slapped them on others, but because we resemble them too, if you know what I mean! We are charged with evil thoughts and deeds. We are guilty of wicked words that have come from our lips as we cast judgment upon others. And how do you think the Judge will find us? Guilty as charged?

Let's take a look at this nugget from God's Word of grace for an answer: "There is therefore now no condemnation for those who are in Christ Jesus. For the law of the Spirit of life has set you free in Christ Jesus from the law of sin and death" (Romans 8:1–2).

Because Jesus steps in and takes on our guilt and shame, and carries it to the cross, we are set free—just like the adulterous woman. We are no longer condemned to death by the Law for our sin, although we deserve it. By faith, we, too, are forgiven in Christ, who died in our place to pay the penalty for our sins and give us the hope of eternal life in His name. We step out with repentant hearts, skipping down the road to our future, free from who we have been or what we have done, knowing that our identity is found in Him.

As Jesus rebuked those who stood in judgment of the woman that day, so He teaches us to give others the same grace He gives. He rebukes us for standing in judgment of others without first examining and repenting of our own shortcomings.

Once again, we climb the mountain with a crowd of Jesus' followers to consider the portion of His Sermon on the Mount that He devotes to this very topic. In those days, just as today, people were prone to judgmental attitudes against others. Let's check out His words:

> Judge not, that you be not judged. For with
> the judgment you pronounce you will be judged,
> and with the measure you use it will be measured
> to you. Why do you see the speck that is in your

brother's eye, but do not notice the log that is in your own eye? Or how can you say to your brother, "Let me take the speck out of your eye," when there is the log in your own eye? You hypocrite, first take the log out of your own eye, and then you will see clearly to take the speck out of your brother's eye. (Matthew 7:1–5)

Jesus is not saying that we should never confront another believer with God's Law, but that we should do so only *after* carefully examining our own hearts and motives; then we proceed gently and out of love for them. The "speck" and the "log" (I love this illustration!) provide a powerful word picture as Jesus illustrates how ridiculous it would be for us to point out the sins of another when we have not first repented of our own. Only then, He tells us, we can confront our brother in love.

This is a tall order for someone (like me) who struggles with a judgmental attitude. And I certainly cannot take even one small step on my own. But because He works tirelessly in me, first covering me with His mercy and forgiveness, I am able to step out from behind my diving board where I stand in judgment (accessorized with my label maker), and move out in my Savior's love to an edgy place, where I am able to give the same grace I receive as I gently admonish others in love.

A Stepping-Out Story

Many of us hear dreadful stories of the stereotypical mother-in-law: Critical. Judgmental. Hurtful. In nightmarish scenes of movies and sometimes in real-life accounts, we witness a daughter-in-law trying to live up to her mother-in-law's expectations, only to fail because she never stood a chance in the first place.

My friend Karen lived through such a nightmare with her mother-in-law, Faye. From the start, Faye labeled Karen as lacking, and she was quick and consistent in her judgment, slapping on this label and others. Karen felt that Faye didn't accept her as a member of the family and that she was never good enough in her roles as wife to Faye's son and mother to Faye's grandchildren. She felt that she could never do anything right in Faye's eyes.

Painful memories for Karen include her interactions with Faye aboard a houseboat on vacations to Lake Powell every summer. This annual family tradition involved several of Karen's in-laws, as well as her immediate family. The experience was a lot like camping, as six to fourteen people shared cozy quarters for two weeks aboard one small floating vessel. Karen was always anxious about bringing her young children to vacation on the water for such a long period of time. Her concerns and responsibilities, coupled with her relationship with Faye, made this family vacation a particularly difficult time for Karen. Unpredictability abounded onboard a boat. There were weather problems, refrigeration concerns, and water-safety issues, and she was responsible for packing, food preparations, sleeping arrangements, and more.

Karen desperately needed her mother-in-law's support, encouragement, and help during those stressful times aboard the boat. Faye helped by playing with the children.

But support and encouragement? Not at all. In fact, Faye did quite the opposite. Karen felt that no matter what she did, Faye criticized her. From making biting remarks about what the kids ate and when Karen fed them, to hurling cruel comments against her in front of the other people on the boat, Faye was continually labeling her. Karen remembers, "My survival method was to put on my life jacket, get a good book, and swim as far away from her as possible so her words could not burn me."

And then there was the coffeepot. Every morning, Faye would get up extra early and bang the coffeepot around as she made the morning brew, rousing everyone much earlier than necessary. Karen was certain this was done as yet another attempt to exasperate her. Finally, there was the food. Faye often planned the meals on the boat, guaranteeing a plethora of food that was ridiculously far beyond the amount that was needed. At the end of the trip, someone had to repack all of it, carry it off the boat, and haul it home. While this may seem like a minor inconvenience, in the process of transporting bulky port-a-cribs, diapers, and life jackets, as well, the extra food was the straw that broke the camel's back for Karen.

The remainder of the year, off the boat, was no different. Karen recalls, "I would like to say that other times with Faye were better, but for the most part it was more of the same from my mother-in-law: I was not accepted; I was not good enough. I heard more hurtful words." There were times she just couldn't take Faye's treatment and she would enter into a bitter battle of the tongues with her mother-in-law. Karen felt like a hypocrite when she could not show love, kindness, and forgiveness to the very person from whom she so desperately sought it.

Karen prayed fervently that God would help her be a better daughter-in-law. She kept thinking that somehow if she just tried harder, she could be good enough in Faye's eyes and that as a result, Faye would come to like her and treat her kindly instead of critically.

Then one year while vacationing on the boat, it was clear that something was not right with Faye. When they returned home, Karen and her husband immediately took Faye to the doctor. Faye's diagnosis was lung cancer with metastasis to the brain. Karen courageously joined her husband in an invitation to Faye to live in their home. At first, Faye was resistant, saying she would be infringing upon them. But thanks to their combined encouragement, along with the doctors', she finally consented and moved into their house. Karen remembers, "Initially, I was anxious, but I knew that God was calling me to open my heart and home to her." The previous summer, Karen and her sisters had cared for their mother during her final battle with cancer. She knew that God had prepared her for the task ahead.

In the seven remaining weeks of Faye's life, God answered many of Karen's fervent prayers with a resounding yes! and He opened her eyes to so much more. Her family's time with Faye was richly blessed. They enjoyed what Karen calls a "seven-week party" filled with many fun family meals, lots of laughter, and a multitude of visitors. Most important, the party was filled with moment upon moment of mutual love and acceptance. Karen's husband said that

Faye's demeanor during her final weeks reminded him of life with her during his boyhood days. And Karen was able to see her mother-in-law in a very different light. Their relationship was no longer like something out of a nightmare but was more like a dream come true.

Shortly after the diagnosis, as Karen was taking Faye to a doctor's appointment, Faye spoke up. "I've tried to be good and do the right thing my whole life." She had been a devout church woman but did not grasp the truth of God's grace.

Karen replied gently, "Faye, you have tried to do and be good your whole life, but no one can be perfect. That's why we rely on God's grace through Jesus Christ. That's why Jesus lived a perfect life and then died on the cross to pay the price for our sins."

I've tried to be good. Hadn't Karen thought the same thing in regard to her relationship with Faye? *If I just tried harder.* But they were both found lacking; they had both fallen short.

Because of our sin, we all fall short in our relationship with God and in our relationships with one another. No matter how hard we try, we can never be good enough. "For all have sinned and fall short of the glory of God" (Romans 3:23). But get this: by God's amazing grace, we *are* good enough—even perfect—because He sees us through Christ. "And are justified by His grace as a gift, through the redemption that is in Christ Jesus" (v. 24) Imagine that label, placed squarely over all the rest: Good Enough. Or better yet: Made Perfect in Christ.

Karen asked Faye if she could read to her from *Portals of Prayer* the same devotions that she had read to her mother as she was dying the previous year. With tears, Karen shares, "They were absolutely wonderful! They so clearly pointed to God's grace and also to His peace at times like this. Faye was receptive and appreciative of every devotion I read to her." Shortly thereafter, Faye went home to be with Jesus.

During Faye's final days, Karen received an incredible gift as she was able to witness Faye stepping out of the judgmental attitude she had displayed toward her. However, this isn't really a stepping-out story about Faye. It's about Karen. She realized she had been guilty of judging the very person whom she felt had judged her so critically. She responded to Faye's labeling of her by giving Faye labels as well: EXASPERATING (the coffeepot wake-up calls) and RIDICULOUS (the overabundant provision of food), just to name two.

Nine years after Faye's death, while vacationing again on the houseboat, Karen learned a couple of facts about her mother-in-law that she had never known before. God has used these to further soften her heart, enabling her to see Faye no longer through judgmental eyes but through a lens of grace.

• Why was her mother-in-law so uptight while they were on the boat? Karen learned that Faye was so deathly afraid of water that she didn't even like to take a shower at home, so joining her loved ones, children, and grandchildren on the water for two weeks must have been an anxiety-ridden ordeal for her.

• In the earlier years of their houseboat vacations, some of Faye's family members were struggling with financial difficulties. The extra food was her inconspicuous way of providing for them by sending the spare food home with her family.

As far as Faye's ongoing criticism of her daughter-in-law, yes, she judged unfairly at times. She slapped on labels that she should not have. With greater understanding today, however, Karen admits that as her boys have grown and now have girlfriends, she has become more sensitive. Her mom heart is tweaked when one of her boys is hurt by a young woman. She is starting to see life through her mother-in-law's perspective, understanding that perhaps what she saw as a critical woman was really a protective mother who simply did not want to see her son or grandsons get hurt.

Karen remembers her mother-in-law with great fondness now, and is so thankful for the time God gave them together during Faye's final days. Jesus gently led her to step out of her judgmental attitude toward Faye and give her the same grace that she is given freely by God in Christ. FORGIVEN. FREE. MORE THAN "GOOD ENOUGH."

Life on the Edge

While my old label maker was able to impress a word or phrase firmly onto the sticky-backed tape, God impresses—even permanently engraves—a word on His hand. Not just any word. It's my own name. And yours too. As He proclaimed to the nation of Israel, so He declares to you and me: "Behold, I have engraved you on the palms of My hands"

(Isaiah 49:16). He has compassion on us; He will not forget us. Ever. We are His chosen and redeemed children in Christ Jesus, forgiven and set free to live our lives on the edge.

Yes, again, Jesus leads me to a life on the edge. Of course, this doesn't mean that I won't fall backward into that place of judgment behind the board, but that He holds me in His grip and gently leads me back out. Ah, grace! It is only by His grace that I want to put the best construction on a fellow child of God. Instead of looking upon that person in judgment, I can look upon him or her with my Savior's love. Since the old label-making methods have gone out the window, I no longer need an excuse to exclude, a defense to avoid discussion, or a reason to justify judgment toward them. I know that Jesus lovingly labels them with His grace, and I can too.

Remember the A list I so conveniently conjured up in my mind? Living on the edge, Christ empowers me to flip the list over and look at it completely backward and upside down.

People's **appearance** simply means to me that they have appeared before me, not by accident, but because they have been placed in my path—perhaps for just a moment, but maybe for much longer. I remember that God looks on them with love no matter what the world thinks of their appearance. And maybe my kind words or generous actions will be the first they have seen for a long time.

I may have little or no evidence of the **assumptions** that I make about someone. So I rely only on what I know to be true: I assume she has needs, just as I do. I assume he is forgivable and reachable, just as I am. I assume she needs to know that she has a Savior who loves her; I know I do. How can I touch another life based on these special assumptions?

When I consider a person's **associations,** I think of my Savior, who associated Himself with everyone, even those whom the world had judged or cast aside. Wow! These people were associated with Jesus Himself! Instead of judging someone as guilty by association, I remember that he or she is loved by Christ, who freely forgives. I can point her to the cross, that she may be free by association in Christ Jesus.

Reflections

1. Click, click, click. What kind of labels has your label maker created lately? Have you mentally slapped a judgmental label on someone recently and then walked away? Share.

2. Have others labeled you unfairly? With what words have you been judged? Envision Christ completely covering those hurtful labels with His label of grace for you. What words do you think He would choose? (See Isaiah 43:1; John 15:15; and 1 John 3:1 just to get you started.)

3. Read John 8:2–11. As you do, slip your feet into the ordinary sandals of a person in the crowded courts that day. You came to hear Jesus teach at the temple, only to be disrupted by this commotion. You see the accusers' sneers. You hear their charges against *her,* the adulteress. And then you witness an amazing turn of events. What is your response? How might Christ's words and actions impact or change you?

4. Jesus steps in to set us free from the condemnation and death that we deserved for our judgmental attitude against others and every other sin. Praise Him right now with a repentant and thankful heart!

5. Stepping out of our judgmental attitudes does not mean we are never to confront another Christian who is trapped in sin. What does Jesus exhort us to do first? Have you been in a situation recently where you needed to call someone to question about a sin? Examine your heart and your motives first. Repent of your own sinful ways. Then prayerfully step out in Jesus' strength to speak the difficult truth in love.

6. Maybe you have something similar to my A list (judging by appearance, assumption, and association, or the like). How can you turn that list upside down and backward to see a person—one whom you were getting ready to judge—in a whole new light? Ask the Holy Spirit to guide you.

7. What might your life on the edge look like as you step out of your judgmental attitude, by the Spirit's power, into a place of grace, where Christ would have you live?

Write further
reflections here

CHAPTER NINE

Stepping Out of My Hurried Lifestyle to a Life of Balance and Rest

Be Still

It was a lovely little restroom, tucked between the lobby and the lounge of a beautiful resort. I had accompanied my husband to a church workers' conference, happy to take advantage of the opportunity to get away from my busy schedule and unwind for a few days.

While my husband attended meetings, I was on my own to explore the resort complex. During a stroll, enjoying the relaxed pace and the welcome break from my hurried life that affected even the most basic necessities, such as restroom time, I ducked into the small restroom. Uninterrupted. No one hollering, "Is dinner ready yet?" No one holding me to a schedule. No dog barking, no phone ringing, no soup boiling over on the stove.

Then, in the middle of my restroom respite, everything went black. I was engulfed in sudden and complete darkness. I couldn't see a thing. Blinking hard, I wondered for a moment if I had gone blind. Then I guessed that perhaps the power had gone out. I sat completely still, listening for commotion in the lobby. I heard nothing out of the ordinary. Oh dear. What could be wrong? As I sat in panicked silence, my mind raced through options. Should I call out for help? How was I going to make my way out of here and to my room? If I was blind, I was going to need to learn to feel for things in the dark, right? So I slowly reached out my hand. And *presto!* Light flooded the small room once again. The motion-sensitive light switch was triggered by the movement of my hand.

All at once, three emotions hit me: relief (I was not blind, after all!), embarrassment (I mean, really! I had panicked over a motion-sensitive light that was just doing its job), and humor (For obvious reasons, the giggles hit me hard! I almost wanted to tell my story to the front desk staff. Almost.)

All this happened because I actually sat still long enough for the lights to go out. Amazing! That would never happen at home, would it? Not likely, since 1,500 tasks vie for my attention on any given day, and I must be on the move if I want to accomplish them. My to-do list gets longer and longer as I overcommit myself, placing unrealistic expectations on myself and on my time. (Let's face it, most days, the only time I am completely still is when the lights *are* out, because it's the middle of the night and I'm asleep!) Was the Lord using my silly incident on this day to remind me to simply slow down? To redirect me to make time for the true respite that only He can give? To step out of my hurriedness and be still before my Savior?

I walked to my room and pondered this. I pulled out my Bible and my journal and I began to write: "Help me to focus on You . . . to be still and let You speak to me . . ." As I sat still, listening for the Lord, He spoke to me through His Word: "Be still, and know that I am God" (Psalm 46:10).

Some seasons of my life have been so marked with hurriedness that I nearly forget what it is like to be still. And I justify the busyness: "But Lord, it is good stuff, and I'm doing it all for You!" Surely, He would want me to say yes to one more thing when it can benefit another person and may even impact a life for Christ. But sometimes more is just more, not better. Even a "good" thing can cease to be good when we are stretched so thinly that we fail to do any one thing effectively.

A former pastor of mine used to say, "If everyone in our church family would do one thing and do it well—for His glory and in His strength—we would never have an unmet need." Does that mean I don't have to be a one-woman army? The truth is that my too-full, ultra-busy, over-extended lifestyle can easily lead to periods of burnout; physical, mental, and emotional stress; and strained relationships. In light of this truth, a hurried lifestyle isn't sounding so good anymore, is it?

Jesus Steps In

In the context of my stillness in the restroom that allowed the lights to go out, perhaps I (and you too?) have been on the move for so long that I wonder what will happen if I actually stop for real rest. Will the "lights go out"? Will I panic? Will I call out for help?

Without God's guiding hand upon our lives, we grope about in spiritual blindness, managing to make our way here and there as we labor, but struggling for lack of direction and failing to find rest. In His amazing mercy, our Lord Jesus steps into our lives and calls us to come to Him; to step out of our hurried lifestyle; to rest in His forgiveness, in His presence, and in His Word. We reach out our hands and *presto!* His light floods the darkness, and we realize He was with us all along. He assures us that when we take the time to be still and know that He is God, He will give us real rest.

Jesus said, "Come to Me, all who labor and are heavy laden, and I will give you rest. Take My yoke upon you, and learn from Me, for I am gentle and lowly in heart, and you will find rest for your souls. For My yoke is easy, and My burden is light" (Matthew 11:28–30). For the Jews of Jesus' day, the Law was like a heavy yoke that had been laid upon them. They were wearied by its weight, loaded down with its many rules and regulations, and exhausted in their labor to keep the Law perfectly as a vain attempt to earn salvation.

What could be said of us today? We know we cannot keep the Law perfectly, yet we hurry and scurry to do everything just right, as if we are trying to somehow earn God's favor, only to fall short again and again. How great is the relief we find in Jesus' words! He knows the weight is too much for us to bear, so He takes it from us. Jesus stepped in for us, fulfilling the Law perfectly on our behalf.

We no longer have to labor under the heavy burden of our sin. Christ removed that burden—that death sentence—when He carried our sin to the cross and died for our sins. We find true rest for our souls through the forgiveness He provides. When we are yoked, or joined, with Christ to the Gospel, He gently leads, guides, and teaches us throughout our walk with Him. He is with us now, lightening our loads as we go, giving us daily rest in Him.

Jesus modeled rest. In the middle of a busy and demanding ministry, He made the time for real rest with the Father by waking up early and going away by Himself for a time of prayer: "And rising very early in the morning, while it was still dark, He departed and went out to a desolate place, and there He prayed" (Mark 1:35).

Jesus encouraged rest for the twelve apostles who served under Him during His ministry. In Mark 6:7–13, we learn that He sent them out on a rigorous mission to proclaim a message of repentance, to cast out demons, and to heal the sick. When they returned to Jesus later, they told Him all that they had done and taught. "And He said to them, 'Come away by yourselves to a desolate place and rest a while.' For many were coming and going, and they had no leisure even to eat" (Mark 6:31).

Jesus models and teaches the importance of rest for body and soul. We follow the Lord's lead to make time for rest so we can return to our work refreshed and ready to serve again. We slow down. We pray. We listen to God's gentle, guiding voice as He speaks to us in His Word.

Putting on the Brakes

Why is it that when I am scurrying to an appointment with mere minutes to spare, every single light turns red and the car in front of me travels twenty miles per hour under the speed limit, forcing me to put on the brakes again and again? And, sure enough, every time I am pressed for time because I have squeezed yet another commitment into my day, I run into someone I know. A quick chat puts me behind. So when I ask, "How are you?" do I bother to put on the brakes and listen long enough to hear a reply?

Have you ever been forced to put on the brakes when you were in a hurry? Maybe we should look at these slowdowns as wake-up calls that remind us of the need to change our hurried pace, to open up our schedule, and to create some breathing room. Maybe there is a specific reason for the slowdown, such as a person whose life will be touched by ours, but only when we allow ourselves to come to a screeching halt. How often I have been humbled in the midst of my hurry by someone who steps right in my way!

This happened to me at the grocery store not long ago. An elderly couple was leisurely strolling down the aisle. Right down the *middle* of the aisle. I needed something in that aisle and I was, you guessed it, rushing to get it. The man noticed my cart careening toward him, so he shouted to his wife, "Look out! This lady is obviously in a big hurry!" Ouch. A wake-up call? Maybe. It certainly caused me to put on the brakes so I wouldn't run over any sweet little couples.

Then, on that same shopping trip, just a few aisles over, I ran into an acquaintance. (Not literally, since I had the brakes on.) Feeling more aware following my wake-up call, I stopped to talk with her, and she shared some struggles with me. We talked about our faith, and I felt compelled to give her a devotion book I had tucked in my purse as a day-brightener. Would this have happened if I had maintained my hurried pace? Maybe. But when I focus only on my must-get-done tasks of the day, I speed right past the gifts that may be placed before me, unnoticed and unopened. Did the Lord nudge me to put on my brakes that day?

The writer of Hebrews compares our Christian life to a race. "Let us run with endurance the race that is set before us" (12:1). The race of life that Christ has set before us is not meant to be a sprint. We are not to run as fast as we can (especially when steering a shopping cart), only to find we are winded, exhausted, and unable to keep going. Instead, we look to the race as a long-distance run or a marathon, one in which great endurance is needed. We pace ourselves, guided and trained by our Coach, and we put on the brakes to rest along the way. Life is much richer and sweeter at a less-frenzied pace.

When He created the world, God established a day of rest for our benefit, that we may recuperate from the week's work, reflect on our purpose and the tasks at hand, and find rejuvenation for our bodies and souls before we dive into another week before us. He established the Sabbath day that we may find true rest in Him as we worship Him and allow Him to refill us with strength in the Word and Sacrament, and that we may follow His direction for the next adventure that awaits us.

> Now as they went on their way, Jesus entered
> a village. And a woman named Martha welcomed
> Him into her house. And she had a sister called
> Mary, who sat at the Lord's feet and listened to His
> teaching. But Martha was distracted with much serv-
> ing. And she went up to Him and said, "Lord, do You
> not care that my sister has left me to serve alone?
> Tell her then to help me." But the Lord answered
> her, "Martha, Martha, you are anxious and troubled
> about many things, but one thing is necessary.
> Mary has chosen the good portion, which will
> not be taken away from her." (Luke 10:38–42)

Mary, Martha, and their brother Lazarus were dear friends of Jesus. During His busy ministry, our Lord found rest and fellowship in the comfort and hospitality of their home. As we just read, Martha was preparing to serve the Lord and His disciples in her home. (Can you imagine? The *Lord* in your home for dinner?!) Martha had a servant's heart.

I also have a servant's heart, a gift of the Holy Spirit. I love to serve others, too, in my home and elsewhere. I can so easily relate to Martha as she scurried about, busily making preparations for perhaps dozens of guests. Although her guest list included the Lord Himself, she allowed herself to be "distracted with much serving." I am sure that Martha wanted only the best for her many guests. And so do I! Like Martha, I run around in a state of hurry, allowing myself to become distracted by all the busyness, the preparations, and the work that comes with serving.

I tell myself that I have only the best of intentions. Many of my commitments are directly related to serving. Much of my lifestyle has to do with my care for others; in my home, in my church, and in my community. And I let all these good things distract me. I get so busy and stressed by it all that I find myself grumbling much as Martha did: "Lord, don't You care that I have all these preparations to make for my children? for this volunteer project? for women's ministry? Won't anyone help me? Why do others get to rest while I am busy doing all the work?" I become worried and hurried—distracted—as Martha was, by all the preparations to be made.

Jesus did not scold Martha for what she was doing. After all, she was serving her Lord and His disciples; her preparations were well intended and appreciated. Instead, He gently stepped in to remind her of what was even better. "Martha, Martha, you are anxious and troubled about many things, but one thing is necessary" (vv. 41–42). The fact that He said her name twice implies to me that He spoke with great sympathy and tenderness toward her. Today, in His Word, He tenderly redirects me, as He did then for Martha, by helping me put my priorities in their proper places.

"Mary has chosen the good portion, which will not be taken away from her" (v. 42). Make no mistake; Martha's service to the Lord and His disciples was *good*. But the portion that Mary chose was of eternal value; it was even better. I love the word picture that Jesus gives us here. The "good portion" beautifully compares hearing the Word of God to eating a meal. But unlike food, which will eventually be consumed or taken away, this good portion will last forever.

Today, I live in a world that shouts, "Hurry! Prepare the meal and your home. Prepare for the meeting and the upcoming event. Prepare every last detail. Oh, and prepare a new to-do list to include all these preparations!"

Meanwhile, the Lord whispers, "Prepare!"

And I cry, "But, Lord, I *have* been making all these preparations!"

Jesus steps in and gently says, "You are anxious and troubled about many things, but one thing is necessary." In His quiet power, He nudges me to prepare my heart for Him.

How can we prepare our hearts? Much the way we would prepare our homes for an important guest. For such an occasion, we would spare no effort to get everything in order. For this most-important Guest, we reach into the furthest corners and clean out every bit of dirt and filth—our sins. We cannot clean them on our own. Only by the Holy Spirit's leading can we lay them before our most-important Guest.

We repent of our sins to the Savior of the world, Jesus Christ Himself, whose death and resurrection saved us from our impossible task of removing our own sin. He washes us clean. He then gently calls us to sit at His feet and listen to His teaching; to do the one thing necessary in the midst of our busy lives—spend time daily in His Word and in prayer. And as we do, He takes all of our worries, hurries, and distractions and replaces them with trust, rest, and devotion.

Yes, all too often, like Martha, we let ourselves be distracted by the preparations that must be made. "Just a minute, Lord. I'll sit and read a chapter in the Bible, but first I just need to finish the 582 items on my to-do list." Through the Spirit's leading, we long, instead, to first sit at our Savior's feet as Mary did, and hang on to His every word. Mary's heart was not distracted that day but was fully devoted to Christ.

To be fair to Martha, and to encourage all of us would-be Marthas, it's appropriate here to share some evidence of her great faith. In John 11, following the death of her brother, Lazarus, not only does Martha boldly proclaim that Christ is the Savior, but she is also positive that those who believe in Christ will rise to life on the Last Day. Martha wasn't always as hurried and distracted as she was in the Luke 10 passage. We know from the faith she expressed at her brother's death that she was a devoted believer in Christ.

By the grace of God, we can follow Martha's example of faith. We can trust that Jesus enables us to step out of our hurried lifestyle, to put our distractions in proper perspective, and to devote our attention to our Lord and Savior, seeking Him first and sitting at His feet, asking that He help us find balance and rest.

A Stepping-Out Story

Lisa was passionate about every role in her life: a devoted wife and mom, a talented art teacher and school administrator, an active member of her church, and a strong supporter of community-wide events. She loved to jump in with both feet, using her talents for such things as leading and assisting with school programs, performing in the city's summer musicals, speaking at women's-ministry events, painting sets for her daughter's dance recitals, helping lead children's ministry, supporting her son's hockey team, and more. Lisa was always very busy, running through her days in order to keep up with all her commitments.

A few years ago, she was teaching part-time but was as busy as ever, jumping into as many commitments as she could squeeze in. "I had five million things going on; my life was in major overdrive with busyness!" she said. Then her thirteen-year-old daughter, Josie, became ill. What began as stomach flu led to an ear infection, followed by recurring migraine headaches, stomachaches, unexplained fatigue, anxiety, and a severe rash on her feet. "It got scary pretty quickly!" Lisa recalls. "Josie went from being a highly motivated kid who could do everything she wanted, to a child who missed nearly four weeks of school in a row." The illness persisted for three months.

Lisa was involved in one major commitment after another, and several of them culminated early in her daughter's illness. One day, as she was assisting with the leadership of a special presentation, she had to bring her daughter with her. In the middle of the presentation, she looked at Josie and realized just how ill she was. Lisa realized with a start that they shouldn't be there at all.

That was when Lisa recognized that she had to slow down—a lot. She had to give her daughter's care the higher priority and ask other people to take over some of her commitments. "I sat back and realized in the midst of this chaos that God was telling me to slow down and be there for my family in a way that I had not been in a long time." Lisa had to completely let go of many things that she had been doing; things that were helpful to other people, and some that advanced her own professional development. But after her wake-up call, she began to wonder if all these things were really a part of the Lord's plan for her life or if she had been trying to force opportunities to do good things.

Some of Josie's symptoms were very similar to those Lisa herself had experienced when she was younger. She told herself, *You need to be here for her. You can sympathize not just because you're her mother, but also because you know some of what she is going through.* In the trying weeks that followed, Lisa and her husband took turns staying home and called on Josie's grandparents for additional help. Much time was spent with medical specialists, trying to get to the bottom of the illness. Eventually, Josie was diagnosed with Raynaud's Disease, a narrowing of the blood vessels that can be the body's reaction to stress. Large doses of time and rest were necessary for eventual healing.

Lisa recalls thanking God over and over for His timing, thankful that she was *not* teaching full-time during this time. Since she had relinquished other commitments, she had more time to care for her daughter's needs.

Throughout Josie's lengthy illness, Lisa often felt helpless, at a loss for how to help her child. As the Spirit led her, Lisa cried out to God, and He filled her with His grace and peace. She knew she was a forgiven child of the Father, and she received peaceful reassurance in His provision. She found comfort in the words of Mark 9:22–24, the account of

Jesus healing a boy who suffered from demon possession. Although the malady was very different, the father's anguish and cries for help felt much the same as Lisa's pleas to the Lord for her daughter.

> "If You can do anything, have compassion on us and help us." And Jesus said to him, "'If you can'! All things are possible for one who believes." Immediately the father of the child cried out and said, "I believe; help my unbelief!"

Lisa shares, "How many times during those months did I think, 'Lord, I believe! Please help me overcome my unbelief in your power to heal Josie and to help me let go of the busyness that fills my life.'" Although the recovery was slow, Josie did receive healing. Lisa credits Josie's recovery to answered prayers and time for rest. The Lord led Lisa to a greater trust, enabling her to believe in His plan for her life rather than believing in her own plan, and to step out of her busyness and let Him to take the lead.

The following year, as she began receiving requests for her leadership and involvement in a variety of good things again, Lisa carefully and prayerfully declined many of them. Although it was hard for her to say no, especially when saying yes would have forwarded her professional development, she thought back to the previous year and was reminded of her higher priorities and the wisdom of maintaining a slower pace.

As Lisa looks back on all of this, she knows that God desires her to serve Him through things that don't take her away from her family but still enable her to serve others. "It's great to be open to God's plan!" Lisa says with a smile. "I have learned not to jump ahead and try to force a plan of action, but to allow Him to take the lead in His timing. When I was running around and not being still before Him, I could not see the doors He was opening." The words of Psalm 46:10 are often on her heart: "Be still, and know that I am God." Today, Lisa prays for patience to wait for His plan and for quiet time in His Word to recognize when He opens a door.

Life on the Edge

I pace back and forth, living behind the same-old proverbial diving board and tapping my toes in an inpatient hurry to complete the next item on my never-ending to-do list. But Jesus would have me live otherwise. Because He so faithfully steps in and rescues me from my world of hurry and scurry, I can step out beside Him to a life on the edge, a place of balance and rest.

Balance: On the edge, I am able to find balance.

Prompted by the Holy Spirit, I can seek God's direction for balance between actively doing and quietly being as I carefully consider each commitment concerning family, church, work, community, and beyond.

I can ask for His wisdom in choosing the type and number of commitments I make, in order to be able to serve effectively while keeping my life free from unhealthy levels of hurry and busyness.

I pray that I would be able to show love and priority to those closest to me, keeping my schedule open for them wherever possible.

Rest: On the edge, I find real rest with the Lord.

By His prompting, I can carve out time each day for a most-important appointment with the Lord, to sit at His feet and rest in Him. I prioritize time in the Word and prayer.

I can honor a day of rest that He has established for my good. I worship Him and receive strength through the Word and the Sacrament, and I am refreshed and refueled for the week ahead.

I can pray that I may be a witness for Christ by my actions as I choose "the good portion," a regular time of rest in Him.

Living on the edge, I find rest in His presence, right in the middle of life: "He who dwells in the shelter of the Most High will abide in the shadow of the Almighty. I will say to the Lord, 'My refuge and my fortress, my God, in whom I trust'" (Psalm 91:1–2). I reside under the constant care and protection of the Most High—my Father God—who is my Shelter and my Stronghold; my perfect place to find rest.

Reflections

1. Has your hurried lifestyle led to periods of burnout, stress, or strained relationships? Share. Have you been on the move for so long that you wonder what will happen if you actually take a break? Explain.

2. Take a good look at your to-do list, if you have one, or your calendar. Examine your commitments. Is the sheer number of them keeping you in a constant state of hurry? Pray for discernment and clear direction regarding each commitment. Pause to reexamine the number and size of your commitments and adjust accordingly, seeking balance and breathing space.

3. Do you think that your feet are balanced between actively doing and quietly being? Pray that God will help you find the essential balance between activity and rest, between doing and being, between motion and stillness before the Lord.

4. Look again at Luke 10:38–42. Place your feet in Martha's
   scurrying sandals as she took on the great task of serving Jesus and His disciples. Martha's service was a good
   thing. What might have made it better? What was the
   "good portion" that Mary chose? Why could it not be
   taken away from her?

5. Where can you carve out a time each day to rest in Him,
   sitting at His feet and receiving rejuvenation in His Word
   as a first priority? Perhaps first thing in the morning or
   as soon as the kids leave for school? Maybe during your
   lunch hour or just before bed? Commit to a two-week
   period, giving this time a try. If it does not work, choose
   another time of day and commit to two weeks again;
   find a time that works for you! Whom may you call on
   to hold you accountable to this time of rest?

6. How would you choose to spend a full day of rest? What would you do to recuperate, reflect, and find rejuvenation? Give Him your worship and praise in His house, as you are refreshed and refueled in the Word and Sacrament. Here are a few additional suggestions: studying a psalm, making a prayer list, listening to Christian music, sitting still in the Word and listening for God, journaling your insights or prayers, and enjoying a new or favorite devotion book.

7. Recall my former pastor's quote, "If everyone in our church family would do one thing and do it well—for His glory and in His strength—we would never have an unmet need." What is one thing you can do now to meet a need in this world?

8. What might your life on the edge look like as you step out of your hurried lifestyle by the Spirit's power into a place of balance and rest? Where would Christ have you live?

Write further
reflections here

CHAPTER TEN

Stepping Out of My Bitterness and Anger to a Life of Reconciliation and Peace

Crabby Pants

The day began on a sour note. Make that several sour notes. In fact, there were so many sour notes that Sarah was certain the entire day would be off-key. A Lutheran middle school teacher, Sarah usually found great delight and joy in all of the children in her classes as she met with each in turn throughout the school day and in praying with the class they began their time together. But on this particularly warm fall day, the first class was rambunctious, and the second was worse. They were unusually disruptive and disrespectful. *Must be the weather,* Sarah thought. But nothing else seemed to be going right, either. As the day progressed, Sarah found that every person and every little thing was beginning to get under her skin. Ooh, she was angry. Even relatively insignificant things that she may not have even normally noticed grated on her nerves.

Finally, her comparably quieter sixth-grade homeroom class filed into the room. After the students were seated, Sarah marched to the front of the room and announced a warning to them right away. "You may have noticed that I'm wearing my crabby pants today. You're right. I am." Silence. Several sets of wide eyes stared back at Sarah. After a long moment, a quiet, introspective boy raised his hand. "Miss Schultz," he said meekly and sincerely. "Why don't you just change your pants?"

Throughout her frustrating day, Sarah had been praying, "Lord, change my attitude today. Take away my anger and help me see the opportunities of this day through my students." Little did she know that the Lord would bring about His answer through the words of one sweet child. It changed her demeanor for the rest of the day. Later, after the children left, she even got the giggles as she recalled this student's question. Since that day, whenever anger threatens to get a foothold, Sarah prays that the Lord would enable her to change her outlook.

Why do we let those closest to us get under our skin? Why don't we just change out of our crabby pants? We are so easily angered by the people we love. Perhaps it's the children we teach or the adults we work alongside, but most often it's those who live under the same roof with us, or very close by, who irritate us the most. Our husband, children, or parents. Our sibling, roommate, or best friend. Some days (although we might not openly admit it), we are almost looking for them to make a mistake so we can call them on it and have a legitimate reason for our anger against them.

"He is going to tell me one more time how his mom's cooking is better than mine and ask why I can't learn from her. And then I'm going to really let him have it!"

"She is texting again, lying around, listening to music. I bet she didn't get a thing done today. When she comes in here, I'm going to confront her about this!"

"Wait until I show him the credit-card bill and he sees that I know how much he spent! Boy, is he gonna hear about it from me."

Maybe there is something deeper going on underneath. Maybe our quick anger over trivial things, directed toward the ones we love, finds its root in bitter resentment or unresolved anger from past conflicts that we have not resolved.

Or maybe our anger or bitterness has little to do with our closest loved ones, but they end up taking the brunt of it anyway. Maybe outside stressors have left us on edge: work is taking its toll because of too many hours or conflicts with co-workers; we have tough financial decisions to make; a nagging health problem has us secretly upset. And all that bottled-up frustration and stress, though it may not be directly or even indirectly related to our friends or family, comes flying out toward them in sharp, angry tones and words. We are mad and upset about something unrelated, and yet we project it onto our closest loved ones, hurting them in the process.

Struggling to Forgive

Is there a person in your life or a situation in which you are struggling to forgive? Your anger, in and of itself, may not be wrong or misplaced if, for instance, you have witnessed evil or if you were wounded or insulted through no fault of your own. In Ephesians 4:26, Paul restates the words of Psalm 4:4: "Be angry and do not sin." You will experience appropriate anger against evil, injustice, and the sinful acts performed against you and others in this fallen world; but you and I are not to act on our anger in sin.

Paul goes on to say, "Do not let the sun go down on your anger, and give no opportunity to the devil." Although you know you should forgive (hurry, before the sun goes down!), the sting of what he said or the pain from what she did is still raw, whether the offense was earlier today, last week, or even last year. Maybe you are thinking, "I just can't forgive her, not after *that*. It still hurts too much. And besides, she's not even sorry, so I shouldn't have to forgive her." How easily we can wrongly justify our lack of forgiveness and our bitter feelings if we convince ourselves that the other person doesn't deserve to be forgiven.

Sometimes, I become so wrapped up in my hurt feelings that I choose to see only my pain and the anger I harbor against the person who hurt me. "How could she have said those words to me?" "How could he embarrass me that way?" "Have they taken a good look at their own issues?" Stuck in my bitter place, I want only to step out in anger so I can get back at those who hurt me and give them a taste of their own medicine. It's no better when I let the anger simmer for a while. Then it grows to a boil and explodes in ugly words and actions against whoever happens to be near. (Which brings me back to how I often hurt my closest loved ones. *Sigh.*)

Although I want to be able to forgive and seek forgiveness, regrettably, I see myself instead becoming defensive, harboring anger and bitterness, and failing to recognize my own sin, even as I am sinning in my anger against those who hurt me or those closest to me, or both. Sometimes that means sharing all-too-openly with a friend the entire record of wrongs done against me by another. I spew my woes to someone who will listen, trusting she will take my side and affirm my position as the wounded one. Other times, it means conjuring up conversations in my mind with the one who hurt me, setting him straight in the "perfect" conversation that I conceive all by myself, one in which I help him see the error of his ways. (Of course, I don't approach this person in real life; only in my mind.)

It's like keeping an imaginary black book tucked nearby, handy enough to easily pull out and record a mental note of yet another wrong done against me. As I make a mental record of this wrong, I am, in effect, also keeping score. That way, if this person dares to point out a grievance she may have against me, I can pull out my handy-dandy record and bring it against her. *Ha!* I can make sure I get even, or better yet, win.

Yikes! *Win?* What am I saying? I try not to, but I sin in my anger. I let the sun go down on it. I have even allowed the devil to get a foothold. I just can't get past it, and my anger boils over into full-blown bitterness.

Jesus Steps In

My feet are stubbornly stuck at the back of the proverbial diving board. Anger has immobilized me. Stuck in this bitter place, I am not only unwilling, but I am also unable to step out, to move one foot forward on my own. Left to my own devices, I am glued there. And then (praise Him!) my Savior steps in. He comes to me and gently unfastens me, showers me with His grace, and forgives me for my failure to forgive and for so much more! I pour out my hurt and anger onto the One who knows my pain, and He listens. He takes anger away from me and trades it for peace in Him.

Moved by the Holy Spirit, I come before my Savior with a repentant heart, sorry that I could have considered the other person unworthy of my forgiveness when I am clearly unworthy of the Father's forgiveness—yet He pardons me anyway. Christ alone can provide the strength I so desperately need in order to forgive when the pain is raw and the hurt is deep. When I have been severely wounded, it may take me a lot of time to get to that place of forgiveness. It may be a caterpillar's crawl toward the edge, but the Lord is patient and continues His grace-filled work in me, enabling me to step out, if ever so slowly, to forgive the one who hurt me.

What about that imaginary black book where I have kept a record of wrongs? I can let go of it, thanks to Jesus' work in me! By the way, God doesn't have a little black book like this. Although He could count each and every one of our sins against us, and we would be guilty as charged, in Christ Jesus, God not only forgives, but He also willingly forgets. He removes our sins from us "as far as the east is from the west" (Psalm 103:12).

On the Mount Again

Imagine climbing up the mountain to get a good seat, then listening along with the rest of the crowd to Jesus' Sermon on the Mount, as recorded in Matthew 5–7. Anger has been a common problem since the first brothers, and it has continued throughout all of time. Jesus devoted a portion of this important day to the topic:

> You have heard that it was said to those of old, "You shall not murder; and whoever murders will be liable to judgment." But I say to you that everyone who is angry with his brother will be liable to judgment; whoever insults his brother will be liable to the council; and whoever says, "You fool!" will be liable to the hell of fire. So if you are offering your gift at the altar and there remember that your brother has something against you, leave your gift there before the altar and go. First be reconciled to your brother, and then come and offer your gift. (Matthew 5:21–24)

One thing the Jewish authorities—the scribes and the Pharisees—were really good at was teaching the Law to the people. Jesus' followers, the people who were perched all around Him on the mountain that day, had certainly heard "You shall not murder." They knew that murder was against the Law and was punishable in court. Then Jesus came to them, teaching with even greater authority—God the Father's authority—as He explained the fuller meaning of this commandment.

Just as Jesus spoke to them that day, so He also tells us that we have broken the Law against murder if we harbor anger against a brother, a fellow believer. Insults and malicious words are also deserving of God's judgment. Bitterness and simmering resentment are against God's Law. Holding on to unforgiveness, no matter how much we think we are justified in doing so, is a violation of the command against murder.

Jesus' message carries a lot of weight, doesn't it? He tells us that we are, in effect, killing a brother or sister in Christ with our hateful, angry words.

Then Jesus talks about the gifts we offer at the altar; the gifts we bring before the Lord—offerings of worship or prayer, offerings of our spiritual gifts and tithes, all to be used for His glory. He says if we remember that another believer is angry or upset with us, we are to leave our gifts there and go to be reconciled to him or her. We are to do this immediately and earnestly seek restoration in our relationship. Only then should we return to offer our gift before the Lord.

These are difficult words to hear. When I look at this law initially, I may gloat for just a bit, thinking I have this one mastered. I've never actually murdered anyone. But then I learn from Christ's teachings that murder includes anger—and I'm sunk. I am convicted by my sinful anger. I deserve His divine judgment. *How often do I hold a grudge against someone, throw insults in her direction, or spit malicious words in her face? Do I seek reconciliation with other Christians?*

Uh oh.

I don't like my answers to any of these questions. These, like all, sins separate us from God. There is a deep chasm between God in His perfect holiness and us in our sinful wretchedness. (I don't even like writing that word, but it is fitting for our condition.) There is no way for us, on our own, to cross that chasm, to close that gap. No way.

Reconciled!

But I have Good News! There is hope for me, and there is hope for you too. Real hope. Eternal hope. *Salvation* hope. We have that hope because Christ comes to us in the midst of our anger. The very fulfillment of the Law, Jesus Christ, comes to us because He knows we are stuck where we are. We cannot keep this law or any other with the perfection that God requires. Jesus steps in, offers reconciliation with God, bridges the chasm between us by His sacrificial work on the cross, and brings us the hope of salvation.

On the day of Jesus' crucifixion, in the moments following our Savior's final breath, a number of miraculous events took place: the earth shook, the sky went dark in the middle of the day, and "the curtain of the temple was torn in two, from top to bottom" (Mark 15:38). The heavy curtain in the temple had separated the place of worship from the Most Holy Place—the place where the covenant of God was kept. Only the high priest was allowed to enter the Most Holy Place, and then on only one day a year, to sprinkle the blood of sacrificed animals on the mercy seat to atone—forgive—the people of their sins. For centuries, the people had been veiled from the direct presence of God, able to approach Him only through an intercessor, the high priest.

At the hour of Christ's sacrificial death, following this most incredible display of God's extravagant grace, the curtain in the temple was torn in two to reveal to all of God's people that we, repentant sinners, can enter directly into God's presence by the blood of Christ. We are fully reconciled to our Creator.

And because we are reconciled to God by His amazing grace at work in us, we are able to reconcile with one another. Yes, it's true—reconciliation with others is possible in Christ. When we understand how much He forgives us, we are then able to humbly seek another's forgiveness, and perhaps even more amazing, we are able to forgive others for their sins against us too. We can address the reason for the anger and the hurt, assess the damage, get it out in the open, and seek forgiveness. Perhaps both parties are to blame, and both need the soothing, healing balm of forgiveness. This is possible as we delve into God's Word to seek His wisdom, direction, and truth. We address forgiveness scripturally with the Lord's help: "Let all bitterness and wrath and anger and clamor and slander be put away from you, along with all malice. Be kind to one another, tenderhearted, forgiving one another, as God in Christ forgave you" (Ephesians 4:31–32).

We look to the Lord for courage to seek the assistance of a trusted Christian friend or counselor who will walk with us in the Word during those times when we cannot resolve conflict without the help of others. Our relationships, whether with family members or close friends, coworkers or people in the church, are worth the extra work that successful restoration may require. God may use conflict in our closest relationships to bring people to an even stronger place than they were before.

In His name, we can pray for softened hearts toward the ones who hurt us and for eyes to see this woman and that man as they are: children of God who have made mistakes. Trapped in sin, they may not even realize the extent to which their words or actions have hurt us. We can respond intentionally to them only after we have thrown out our black book and grabbed hold of God's Word, stepping out by our Savior's strength as a peacemaker. This is not merely a superficial kind of peace, where everything appears good again while we still seethe and simmer underneath. No, this is the real, only-possible-with-God kind of peace. His extravagant grace is at work in each of us, enabling us to seek this kind of peace.

Seventy-seven times

Let's take another look at God's Word. Jesus taught His disciples peacemaking as He spoke again about forgiveness in Matthew 18:21–22: "Peter came up and said to Him, 'Lord, how often will my brother sin against me, and I forgive him? As many as seven times?' Jesus said to him, 'I do not say to you seven times, but seventy-seven times.'" Called to be peacemakers with our brothers, Jesus teaches that our forgiveness should have no limits. "Seventy-seven times" doesn't mean we stop; it means our mercy should have no end.

Jesus follows these words with a parable about a king who has compassion on his servant, forgiving him for a tremendous debt that the servant could never possibly pay. That same servant turns around, only to mercilessly demand payment from a fellow servant who owes him thousands of times less than he had owed the king. Our heavenly Father has forgiven us for an incomparably greater debt than we will ever be asked to forgive of another. By His grace, we are not like the first servant. We willingly forgive, not because the other person deserves it, but because we didn't deserve the forgiveness Christ freely gave to us on Good Friday.

A Stepping-Out Story

Nicole has a lifelong best friend. Growing up, they did everything together. They shared long talks, secrets, and life experiences. When they were twelve, Nicole's friend was there for her and completely understood as she went through the changes of becoming a woman.

The feelings of growing up, physically, were freshly exciting for timid Nicole. No longer shopping in the children's section of the store, she was beginning to fit into the fashions designed for young women. It was a giggly growing-up girls' time of trying on newly needed undergarments and feeling feminine and special. This is a memorable once-in-a-lifetime stage of a woman's life.

But just as the realization of having this wonderfully new, growing-up, young-woman's body was starting to sink into Nicole, her joy and innocence were irretrievably snatched away. A trusted twenty-year-old family acquaintance liked the new woman Nicole was becoming too. For months, he took advantage of every opportunity to be alone with her so he could use her for his own sexual exploration and gratification. She tried to fight him off, but that just seemed to encourage him all the more, so she ended up stonily enduring. There was never any intercourse, but the fondling, probing, and looking were unwanted and terrifying to Nicole.

She confessed these horrible physical and emotional real-life nightmares privately to her best friend. Ever loyal, her friend shared her anger and turmoil, stayed right by her side, and kept her confidence, all the while comforting her. Nicole told no one else about what was happening to her because, as young as she was, she feared retribution and the stigma that was often attached to these little-talked-about acts.

"As a result," Nicole recalls, "I suffered through the blackness of insecurity and depression for years. My friend tried to help, but I felt worthless and closed in on myself. There were times I pushed my friend's advice aside. Other times, I struck out at my friend with angry words like, 'Why did this happen to me?' I didn't really like me very much, but my friend kept telling me that I was loved and I was special."

As time went on, Nicole was able to work through her anger and hurt to see and accept the fact that she wasn't the one who had done wrong. Thanks to her friend's help, she saw how sin had driven this man to do what he did. She was just the tool he thought he needed—and used—for his sick self-gratification. Nicole's best friend had been with her through it all, holding her up and remaining faithful, even during the most difficult times when she ignored her friend's advice and struck out accusingly in anger and bitterness.

Her friend helped her to see how desperately she needed to remain close to *Him*. Yes, Nicole's lifelong, faithful, and best friend was and still is Jesus. "Without Jesus in my life and by my side, I probably would not be here today."

Brought up in a Christian home, baptized and confirmed in the faith, Nicole rejoices and thanks God that she was given the lifeline of faith from the beginning. Jesus stepped into her life and never left her side. "I prayed, yelled, screamed, and cried to my best friend. He comforted and sustained me throughout that dark time." Church, Sunday

School, and prayer were her tools for healing, as God's Word provided therapy and restoration for her deep emotional wounds.

Years later, after Nicole was married and blessed with children, she was led by the Spirit—compelled by her best friend—to go to this man, to talk to him, and even to *forgive* him. It was then that she found total peace. Her best friend enabled her to step out of the anger and bitterness she had held for so long. She says, "I finally gave up my hold on old hurts and let my emotions and feelings be filled with the soothing balm only Jesus could offer."

This experience shaped Nicole into the faithful Christian woman that she is today, by God's grace. He used the pain of her past to help her have compassion and understanding for those who suffer from the sinful acts of this world. Her best friend walks beside her today and every day, giving her His grace and renewing her strength with the ability to forgive others.

Life on the Edge

I am chosen by God in Christ, and so are you! He calls me to a life on the edge, although in my anger, I would choose to glue myself in place behind that same-old diving board, all the while clutching my imaginary black book. In His mercy, Jesus loosens my feet. Again, He takes me by the hand and leads me to a place where I cannot tread alone, a life of grace and peace toward others.

Living on the edge does not mean I can fix the people who hurt me. It means that because the Holy Spirit lives in me,

I can obey God by offering forgiveness to those who have hurt me, while humbly confessing that the Lord has forgiven me for so much more. I can seek reconciliation and peace. I can, "so far as it depends on [me], live peaceably with all" (Romans 12:18). My response sends a message, loud and clear, of the Savior whom I serve.

In every conflict, I have the opportunity to be a witness—to further His name and shine His light. This can happen only when I let go of my anger and choose to forgive. He gives me the strength to not retaliate when I have been hurt by wounding words or cruel actions, but to respond according to His Word of truth; to respond as Christ would, instead of reacting as the world does. Let's look at another nugget of God's Word of truth on this matter:

> Bearing with one another and, if one has a complaint
> against another, forgiving each other; as the Lord
> has forgiven you, so you also must forgive.
> (Colossians 3:13)

As the apostle Paul closes his Second Letter to the Church in Corinth, he makes one final appeal to the believers: "Finally, brothers, rejoice. Aim for restoration, comfort one another, agree with one another, live in peace; and the God of love and peace will be with you" (2 Corinthians 13:11).

I pray earnestly for God's strength so that I may be able to forgive those who have sinned against me. I ask for His courage so that I may face the people who have hurt me, offering them my forgiveness and aiming for restoration in my relationships with them. I pray that He would help me to live in peace with those around me, showing the same grace to others that He so richly shows to me in Christ, my Savior. He will use my witness to touch others who need to see His grace.

Reflections

1. Do you ever find yourself wearing crabby pants around the people you are closest to? What, in particular, sets you off? Would you admit that some days you have looked for a mistake so that you can claim a legitimate reason for your anger? Explain.

2. Is there a person or a situation in your life in which you are struggling to forgive? With a repentant heart, ask for God's strength to forgive as He has forgiven you, seeking counsel in His Word.

3. Look again at Matthew 5:21–24. As you do, place your feet in the dusty sandals of an unnamed disciple who climbed the mountain with the others to listen and learn that day. Knowing Moses' Law, what might have been this disciple's reaction to Jesus' earth-shattering words about murder and anger?

4. Have you kept something similar to my imaginary black book, a mental record of wrongs done against you? Has it been fun keeping score, or not so much? Ask for the ability to throw it out that you may, instead, seek peace and forgiveness.

5. Read the parable of the unforgiving servant (Matthew 18:21–35). The debt of the first servant was so incredibly high that he could not have hoped to repay it in his lifetime. The debt of his fellow servant was thousands of times less. What does this say of our sin against God in contrast to our sins against one another?

6. Revisit these words from the chapter: "Because we are reconciled to God by His amazing grace, we are able to reconcile with one another." Who comes to mind first when you consider humbly seeking the forgiveness of another? Whom can you forgive, by the Spirit's power?

7. Recall a time when you were hurt and angry but stepped out to forgive. What was the response of others? of the one who hurt you? How did it feel?

8. What might your life on the edge look like as you step out of your anger and bitterness, by the Spirit's power, into a place of grace and peace, where Christ would have you live?

Write further
reflections here

CHAPTER ELEVEN

Stepping Out of

My Comfort Zone to a Life Filled with New Opportunities

The Big Green Monster

Several years ago, we lived in Iowa in a comfy bedroom community outside Des Moines. (You may recall from chapter 7 that this was the very place I did not want to move to.) I was a stay-at-home mom with our three small children in our nice little neighborhood. My hubby's corporate job was nice and stable. We were both very active in our church. We enjoyed great friendships and lived relatively close to our extended family. And life was just plain—you guessed it—*nice*. Predictable. Comfortable. Nice.

In the midst of all this niceness, however, there was something on my husband's heart. I had noticed this for quite a while, and I had a good idea what it was. Still, he had a difficult time admitting it to himself and to me. So he waited until one unforgettable night. Under the protective cover of darkness, he mustered the courage to share these words: "Honey, I believe that God is leading me to go into the ministry."

I had seen it coming. Cory studied God's Word voraciously. He found great joy in writing and leading adult Bible studies for our church. He was passionate about his volunteer ministry roles. On many occasions, Cory and I had even joked about the possibility of full-time ministry work. But this was no joke. As my heart began to race, I rationalized, "Honey, maybe you would like to do some kind of ministry work for a *local* Christian organization."

Patiently, he replied, "No, Deb; I think I need to go back to school."

Still, I was grasping at straws. So I said, "What kind of ministry training do you think is available here in Des Moines?"

He finally had to be very direct with me. "Deb, I think God is leading me to leave my job and leave Des Moines and go to the seminary."

Cory was ready to step out if, indeed, this was God's will. He did not hesitate. He was ready to end a career, move with a wife and three small children, and change our standard of living. Well, *he* may have been ready to step out of our nice little comfort zone, but I wasn't! My husband was asking me to become a pastor's wife, but first, a seminary student wife.

Cory was clear that he would not take this step unless we were in this together, and yet there I was, full of hesitations. In the following months, Cory and I spent a lot of time together talking to God. "Is this really what You're asking of us? Lord, make this abundantly clear if this is what You would have us do. Give us willing hearts and mobile feet to take this giant leap out of our comfort zone into uncharted territory."

During that time, our pastor asked us to participate in an in-depth Bible study requiring daily homework. We tackled it together. Throughout the study, we continued to pray together daily, seeking God's will and a clear path to follow. One pivotal night, Cory's answer came. We were studying Exodus 4—Moses' call from God to deliver His people out of Egypt. The study explained Moses' hesitancy. He did not consider himself a leader or an orator.

"I am slow of speech and of tongue" (v. 10). Moses' words resonated with Cory, a natural introvert who enjoyed the company of a computer more than the camaraderie of co-workers in his daily work. Would he be able to teach and preach, minister and provide care to God's people? The words that followed two verses later, however, were the ones that really stuck with him: "Now therefore go, and I will be with your mouth and teach you what you shall speak" (v. 12). Cory was affirmed that night, receiving peace and clarity of direction from the Lord.

My Savior worked on my heart a great deal throughout our Bible study and prayer time during those months. Jesus stepped in, as He so faithfully does, and gently unfastened my stubborn feet from the safe, comfortable place where they were planted. He took away my hesitation. He even gave me a willing "where you go, I will go" attitude. Because Jesus stepped in, I was able to step out of my nice comfort zone. As the ball began to roll and everything for our milestone move fell into place, I got excited for this life-changing adventure.

Then moving day came. All four of our parents traveled with us, caravan-style, to help us make the major move to a house we had rented sight unseen in St. Louis.

When Cory pulled up to the house in the moving truck, the seminary student in charge of unloading us met him. "Cory Burma?" he asked. "We have a problem." (Our first clue to the nature of events to follow that day.) There had been some miscommunication, and the former resident had not moved out. At all. So we unloaded our entire household onto the driveway in the sweltering August heat. By nightfall, we were finally able to squeeze everything inside.

Inside of *what,* you ask? Our new home was a giant three-story green asbestos-sided structure. Eighty-some years earlier, it had been the neighborhood market. We affectionately referred to it later as "the big green monster." (Our three small children called it "the big green mansion.")

The monster/mansion was a tad smelly, and its interesting interior was in need of a good bath. There were six-foot-tall weeds growing in the monster's yard. We met one of our neighbors when we rear-ended his vehicle on the narrow street, and he told us that another neighbor was under house arrest. But, hey, it was home.

Feeling very disoriented and shaky from the moving ordeal, we trudged forward. We worked hard to prepare beds for all three children and all four parents so they could have some for much-needed sleep. After we got them all settled in bed, it was the middle of the night and time to get ourselves settled. So Cory and I pulled out the sofa hide-a-bed in the center of the dining room floor. (This was the only remaining floor space that night.) Cory crawled into bed, and I looked at him empathetically; his face was tight, and he looked distraught. I sat down to join him, and all at once—*boom!* The bed collapsed upon us, folding us up, completely cocooning us inside!

For a moment, we didn't move. In shock, and now wide awake, we thought perhaps the flooring had caused the sofa to slip and lose its footing. So once we wiggled our way out of the cocoon, we shoved rugs under the sofa's feet. No luck. We adjusted the legs and tried again. In fact, we tried everything we could think of. Three times—*boom!*—the bed collapsed upon us. By then we had the giggles and hoped that the rest of our exhausted family had not been awakened by our crazy commotion. We eventually removed the mattress and laid it on the floor.

I believe that God provided us with this unexpected, silly moment together so we could unwind and make light of the tough new situation in which we found ourselves.

When the giggling ended, we lay there in the dark, and suddenly Cory became very emotional. In the panic and the stress of the day, I had not considered how he was feeling. Back in Des Moines, he had been so certain. He was ready and willing to step out of everything we knew to take this leap into something vastly different to follow what he thought was God's lead. But at that moment, in the middle of our first night in St. Louis, Cory began to question.

"Should we even be here? Was this really God's will, or was this just my crazy idea?" We had just given up everything comfortable and familiar to us to move our family to this place, sight unseen. These were not exactly settling words to lull me to sleep in our new home.

I was desperate. I prayed, "Help, God! Help him to know he is following Your will. Help me, because I don't feel very sure about anything right now either, and we are already here!" I could have blurted out all kinds of things to Cory: how *he* was the one who wanted to move in the first place, that he wasn't the only one feeling afraid. But I didn't. I just held my husband. I cried and I prayed, and I knew that God was going to take care of us, whether we stayed in a nice, safe comfort zone or moved to an adventurous new edge. God would take care of us even in a big green monster.

Fast-forwarding more than a decade, we can look back to God's amazing provision, protective care, and grace that covered us throughout this journey. Our children loved the big green mansion from the start and adjusted immediately to their new surroundings. We came to know and trust a handful of *nice* neighbors; God even opened doors for us to witness to one of them.

Cory thrived at the seminary, and I found my niches in ministry connected to our new church and in the seminary community. *Nice.* Although the years that followed were not without challenge and difficulty, God's purpose prevailed as He used all things for our good (Romans 8:28) and for the growth of His kingdom. The Lord keeps us on our toes as He continues to move us away from our comfort zone and into places and opportunities formerly unknown to us. And each time He leads us to step out of our comfort zone, we grow in faith. We pray for greater faith to follow without hesitation, trusting His lead wherever He may take us.

While much of the world is content to live as though their lives have no purpose beyond their immediate pleasures or comforts, God stirs our hearts to desire more, to hunger for a life that requires us to step out. It would be easy to rationalize that our purpose must be limited to a familiar, comfortable spot. But the Lord calls Christians—you and me—to walk a different walk that may take us to points unknown. To dive right in, to swim upstream, to be *in* the world but not *of* the world. Jesus steps into our hearts and our lives, enabling us to step out of our comfort zones and into the wild and wonderful adventures that await as we follow Him. Our greatest purpose is that we may glorify our Lord and Savior, following Him and fishing for men.

Fishermen Fishing for Men

Way back in chapter 1, when tackling the topic of fear, I talked about four fishermen, and I have referred to them separately several times since: Peter, Andrew, James, and John. Let's take a step back to look at their lives just before they met Jesus.

Theirs was a lowly occupation, a simple trade. Day after day, they boarded their boats, dragging large fishing nets with them, anticipating their next catch. This day was probably like most. Standing near the shore, preparing their nets, they were probably talking about the weather. Not just idle chit-chat, but important dialogue concerning the next catch and the day's work. Were the skies stormy or clear? Was the water choppy or calm?

Likely, their trade had been handed down from generation to generation. The family business; a way of life. Predictable.

Comfortable. Common. They certainly were not nobility, and their lives were far from luxurious, but their simple life was a constant. That is, until one memorable day when Jesus stepped into their world. With perfect purpose and specific intent in every step, Jesus walked along their little portion of the shore of the Sea of Galilee. And as He walked, He called out first to Simon (Peter) and Andrew, "Follow Me, and I will make you become fishers of men" (Mark 1:17).

Can you picture these fishermen at that moment? Did they stare at each other incredulously, wondering what Jesus' words meant? With this simple statement, Jesus rocked their world, asking these fisherman to step out of their boats, out of the world they knew, where they fished for fish. And as He did, He asked them to step into the great unknown, where they would fish for *people*. Did they hesitate? Scripture doesn't tell us that they did. Mark records that they obeyed; that they abandoned their work and took off after Jesus. The very next verse says, "Immediately [no hesitation!] they left their nets and followed Him" (v. 18). Apparently, James and John were down the shore just a bit, fishing with their father, Zebedee. Again, Jesus called out. Again, there was no hesitation. They left their father, the boat, and the family business. They dropped everything to follow Him.

I am afraid that I would have hesitated. I think I would have asked for clarification, details, an agenda. That is so like me. "Okay, Jesus, but I would like to know a few things first. What is the plan, and where are we going? I'm not sure I am comfortable stepping away from my nets and out into the unknown. And just what do you mean by "fishers of men" anyway? How will this work, exactly?"

These soon-to-be disciples were simply obedient to His call. Even when that meant leaving everything that was comfortable and common to them, even when that meant stepping away from their livelihood and tradition and family. The fact that Jesus chose them at all is amazing in itself. Hardly theologians, not even close to being experts in the Jewish law, they were simple men of trade. And yet He *did* choose them.

Jesus Steps In

Today, He chooses you and me right where we are. Jesus steps in and says, "Follow Me." He calls us to step out of our collective comfort zones to go where He leads, to be committed—as the first disciples were—to follow Him above all things. While we may remain businesswomen, teachers, homemakers, wives, mothers, and more, we are Christ followers first.

In our sin, however, some days we hesitate; other days we simply fail to follow altogether. We are not committed. We fail to place Him first. We shrink back and huddle into our nice little comfort zones, content to stay just where we are. But God doesn't let us stay there, huddled in our zone. He knows we cannot step out on our own, so He comes to us in the midst of our sin.

Through Christ, God forgives us for our hesitation and our failure to follow. He fills us with the Holy Spirit, enabling and empowering us to trust and step out. Because the Holy Spirit has gifted us with faith, we can follow the Lord just as the disciples did—without hesitation, clinging to His every Word, going where He leads, serving each person He places in our path, trying something new, exploring a gift or talent, and reaching out in His name.

Stepping out of our comfort zone and following our Savior to a life on the edge may not require a physical or geographical move on our part. It may not require a step out of America and onto foreign soil. It may not even mean taking a step outside of our community. Maybe our occupations stay the same. Maybe our neighborhoods are the same. And maybe our church home is too. But our purpose, as Christ reveals it to us with increasing clarity, changes us and permeates every part of our lives. We step out for Him in our workplaces; we courageously cast nets in our neighborhoods; we fish for men and women and children who have yet to meet the Savior; we fish for those who desperately need to know Him and what He has done for them.

The message of grace and salvation Christ shared with His disciples was the same message He led them to share with the world. The disciples' journey was not an easy one. Each step took them to new people and to different challenges, through many obstacles and into frequent persecution.

Their journey is ours. Oh, sure, today it looks different. The people are different. But challenges are not so different. We also face obstacles in the form of resistance and denial; we may even be persecuted. And Christ's message of grace and salvation is the very same. In our homes, communities, and places of work, whether we remain in familiar surroundings or make a major move, we serve others and give the Good News of our Savior to them. We may not be theologians or degreed Bible scholars. But simple people like you and me can be emboldened by the Holy Spirit to simply share our faith. And we do so courageously by God's grace, even when that means overcoming obstacles that may threaten our ability to reach out with His saving love. We are fishers of men!

Stepping out of our comfort zone means yielding our life to Him. It means putting our life in His hands and trusting Him to provide and protect, even as He leads us into uncharted territory. On the back end of the diving board, it seems more comfortable to attempt to retain complete control over our lives (as if *that* were possible). But out there on the edge, it is incredibly freeing to just let go and let the Lord take over. He gave up His life for us. In response, we can drop everything to place Him first and follow Him. And we pray that others might see our lives yielded to Christ and be drawn to Him as a result.

A Stepping-Out Story

Several years ago, my friend Shelly came across a Christian newspaper called *Nebraska Family Times.* At the time, she was promoting a self-published book, so she decided to email the editor of the paper to ask if she would review the book. In her reply, the editor invited Shelly to write news articles for the monthly publication. An avid writer, Shelly was thrilled with the opportunity. After a while, she was also asked to write feature articles for the paper.

Imagine Shelly's surprise when, a few years later, she received an inquiry from the same editor, asking if she would like to purchase the newspaper. Health and family issues were prohibiting the current editor from continuing to publish the paper.

Shelly says her first response was, "I could *never* do that! I know nothing about owning or publishing a newspaper!" She recognized she had a God-given gift and passion for writing. She possessed an equally great desire to encourage people in their faith walk through that writing. But she never dreamed that the Lord would open a door for her to use these gifts and passions to this extent or in this direction. *How would the paper get printed? Who would handle the layout? What about deadlines? contributors? publicity? And could she pay the bills?* Questions and unknowns flooded her mind. But excitement and anticipation began to build as she considered the possibilities that lay before her in this proposed venture. When she shared the opportunity with her husband, he encouraged her to give it a try, telling her it would be a perfect fit. After much prayer and consideration, asking for God's clear direction, she purchased the newspaper and took the reigns as publisher and editor.

Stepping out of her comfort zone, following her Savior's lead to a life on the edge, Shelly's fears began to fall away as she received a wealth of great information from the former owner to help her get started. The printer, who continued to work with the paper's layout, was equally helpful and provided a great deal of flexibility, understanding, and patience, working with Shelly as she learned and sometimes waiting patiently for bills to be paid.

As you might guess, the blessings and benefits of this venture have gone far beyond learning how to run a newspaper and how to manage the many details that come with it. Shelly's trust in the Lord's provision has grown a great deal in the years that have followed, as she has seen Him faithfully provide the necessary means to pay all the bills, even during months when she wondered how financial ends could possibly come together. "I was the type of person who worried over bills. It was way out of my comfort zone to not know for certain where the money would come from. Now I trust God, believing the money will be there to pay the bills when I need it. He has never failed me!"

The Lord impressed upon Shelly's heart the desire to tithe at least 10 percent of the net proceeds of the paper (another opportunity to step out). Posted on her office bulletin board is this passage, reminding her of God's grace as she gives with a grateful heart:

> The point is this: whoever sows sparingly will also reap sparingly, and whoever sows bountifully will also reap bountifully. Each one must give as he has decided in his heart, not reluctantly or under compulsion, for God loves a cheerful giver. And God is able to make all grace abound to you, so that having all sufficiency in all things at all times, you may abound in every good work. (2 Corinthians 9:6–8)

Shelly knows that God's grace abounds. She shares with humble trust, "God has been faithful. He always keeps His promises!"

More blessings and benefits have poured in through readers' responses. "I am so encouraged when I hear that an article I printed, or the whole paper, has touched or encouraged someone." Countless people have been inspired through the paper's articles and news stories, devotions, and Scripture posts.

Shelly was not done stepping out of her comfort zones when she courageously took over the newspaper and learned the ropes. Since then, she has stepped out many times. While she enjoys promoting Christian news, events, and businesses, God has continued to stretch her comfort level and grow her in unexpected ways while working with authors and contributors, advertisers and sponsors, businesses and organizations. "I don't necessarily enjoy being a salesperson, but I have had to ask for ads, sponsorships, and more."

Several times, she has worked with experts in different areas of publishing, recognizing that she may be a novice by comparison. One expert who was active in other Christian media approached Shelly. The woman began writing a column for the paper and got it involved in several events. At first, things went smoothly. But then she began to be critical and demanding, refusing to have her work edited and insisting that someone else was sabotaging the paper. How was Shelly to handle this? After all, this woman was supposed to be an expert! After much prayer for guidance, Shelly stepped out (again) and very gently confronted the woman, requesting that she take a break.

Another so-called expert was to assist Shelly with technology. The first time they met, he criticized every detail of the paper, from the setup to the advertisements, marking up the paper and berating her personally in the process. Although it was tempting for Shelly to walk away right then and there, she held her tongue and humbly endured his remarks. He helped with the paper for a brief time and then moved on.

Today, Shelly still ponders why these critical people were in her life. These experiences certainly kept her on her toes and out of her comfort zone. She believes that God has used these experiences to teach her several things:

- She has learned to trust Him for confidence in herself and vision for the future of the paper, and not just trust experts without question.

- She has learned not to automatically take criticism, but to look at it humbly and carefully, determining whether it is valid.

- She has been reminded just how important it is to live a Christian life of kindness and patience, especially when working with others.

Shelly realizes now that stepping out of her comfort zone isn't as scary as she first thought, because God is by her side. She prays every day, especially when she is putting together an issue, that God will guide and lead her to material for the newspaper that touches the hearts of readers and encourages them in their walk with Him. She says with a smile, "I'm sure God will ask me to step out of my comfort zone again." She seeks to listen and follow the Lord's will as He continues to lead her to a life on the edge.

Life on the Edge: Make a Move

Living in the center of God's will can be the edgiest—the scariest—place we can be because it may mean stepping out of everything comfortable, convenient, or common. Maybe, as we are called by God to be missionaries in our neighborhood or in another country, it means moving out of the familiar and safe. I would love to tell you that I'm certain I will jump right out of my comfort zone again and again as God shows me the latest diving board and beckons me to follow Him out to the edge of it. Yet, I know that I might stumble, shrink back, and cower in my so-called safe space. But God doesn't leave me there, and I praise Him for that. He takes me by the hand and lifts me up. In His Word, I am given the courage once more to step out there to the edge right next to Him!

Someone once told me, "Say yes when God calls, and you will embark on an adventure." Christ calls each of us to follow Him to a life on the edge, and that means making a move. To make a move *toward* a new opportunity means moving *away* from something else. Does this mean a cross-country U-Haul move or one-way flight to a foreign land for business or mission work? Perhaps. It may mean that you will stay right where you are geographically while still making a major move into the unfamiliar—a new adventure or challenge.

Are you receiving a nudge to go back to school or begin a new job? Maybe God will use the unique combination of your personality and gifts to have you serve someone in need or help in a crisis: Can you provide a meal or offer comfort? Can you fill sandbags or donate blood?

Maybe you are to lead a new ministry or to contribute to an existing one in a new way: Can you teach youth or children? steer a committee? provide care for someone who is housebound? Attend a Bible study for the first time?

Maybe the Lord will lead you to open your heart to someone of a different culture or world-view, or to open your home to someone in need: Can you reach out to the new neighbor or give up your guest room?

Make a move. Say yes and serve when the Lord calls you, and He will be glorified through your service. This is edgy living.

Ephesians 2:10 explains my irresistible desire to step out in my Savior's strength: "We are His workmanship, created in Christ Jesus for good works, which God prepared beforehand, that we should walk in them." God created us for a purpose. He had a plan from the beginning for me to do what I am moved to do now, as I walk in faith, right out here on the edge!

Reflections

1. Share a stepping-out story. Were there difficulties or trials awaiting you when you stepped into the new challenge or place? How have you seen Him use these for good or for the growth of His kingdom? (Read Romans 8:28.)

2. Read Mark 1:16–20, where Jesus calls the first disciples. As you do, place your feet in the seaside sandals of James or John. Imagine hearing Jesus' invitation while working in your boat and stepping out of it, walking away from your father and the family business to follow Him. How can you tell that theirs was likely a large fishing business, able to provide relative future security? What kind of security would they receive as they dropped their nets and followed Jesus?

3. What edgy thing may God be leading you to do today? What may make you hesitate? Is something causing you to shrink back and huddle in your nice little comfort zone? Explain.

4. Ask for God's clear direction and leading in your life right now. Seek His Word for guidance. Then pray for a willing heart and mobile feet to take a leap; to step out to explore a gift or talent, to try something new, and to reach out with your Savior's love.

5. Look back on all the things in your past that God custom-packaged to prepare you for what He is calling you to do now. What things in your past enable you to step out of your comfort zone to a gutsy new thing or a scary new place today? Write them here or share with others.

6. Throughout this chapter, we referred to our nice little safe place as our comfort zone. In reality, our true comfort comes from the Lord, who calms, consoles, and cares for us completely wherever we are called or in whatever we are led by the Spirit to do. Explore just a few of the many verses that point to our ultimate source of comfort: Isaiah 49:13; Jeremiah 31:13; 2 Corinthians 1:3; 2 Thessalonians 2:16–17.

7. What might your life on the edge look like as you step out of your comfort zone and into a new challenge, opportunity, or location where Christ would have you live?

Write further
reflections here

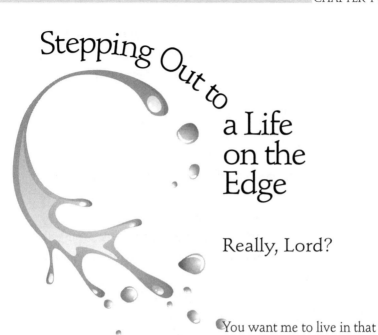

CHAPTER TWELVE

Stepping Out to a Life on the Edge

Really, Lord?

You want me to live in that scary place w-a-y out there on the edge? Are You sure You don't just want me to visit it once in a while and then hurry back to my safe spot on the cement behind the board?

Oh, that's right. You have gone there before me. And now You are calling me to step out beside You and take a stand for You, my Savior. You are calling me to a life on the edge. I don't have to live encumbered by my many sins and shortcomings that trap me back behind the board. Because You step in, by Your grace and in Your strength, I can step out. Thank You!

> For the grace of God has appeared, bringing salvation for all people, training us to renounce ungodliness and worldly passions, and to live self-controlled, upright, and godly lives in the present age. (Titus 2:11–12)

Although I may still struggle in my sin and find myself running back there, cowering behind the board again and again, by Your grace, You continue to come after me. You gently take me by the hand and guide me in Your Word of truth once again, enabling me to live a "self-controlled, upright, and godly" life w-a-y out there on the edge, right next to You.

Lord, You take my hand and lead me gently out of my fear to a place of courage, helping me to fix my eyes on You. You continually lead me to step away from my painful past to live fully in the present. You help me out of my anxieties and my worries, moving me to a place of peace and trust. You grab hold of me and hoist me out of my insecurity, giving me Your confidence. You enable me to turn from my unhealthy need to please everyone, and I am emboldened to live my life for You!

Jesus, You unwrap my heart from around my material possessions, giving me a heart for my heavenly treasure, instead, and filling me with contentment. You remove my towering stack of arrogant pride and selfish ambition so that I can see clearly from a new and humble perspective. You tenderly lift me out of my judgment seat and bring me to a place of grace toward others. You rescue me from my hurried lifestyle, leading me to a quiet space of balance and rest.

Savior, You unglue me from the spot in which I am stuck in my anger and bitterness, and You take me to a place of reconciliation and peace. You pull me out of my safe space—my comfort zone—and You give me the courage to try something new for You! I am free to live my life on the edge, knowing You never let go of Your grip on me.

Jesus, You have given me everything I need to live my life for You. You have moved me to a life on the edge!

We Have Been with Jesus, and We Are Changed!

Two heavy-hearted disciples were traveling from Jerusalem to Emmaus, as recorded for us in Luke 24:13–35. They were grieving over Jesus' crucifixion and the overwhelming events of the previous three days. Confusing reports had just come to them, claiming that Jesus had been seen alive. *What could this mean? Could He really be alive? How could this be?*

They were joined on the road by the resurrected Jesus Himself, but they were kept from recognizing Him during their journey. As Jesus stepped alongside them, hearing of their grief and confusion, He said to them, "'O foolish ones, and slow of heart to believe all that the prophets have spoken! Was it not necessary that the Christ should suffer these things and enter into His glory?' And beginning with Moses and all the Prophets, He interpreted to them in all the Scriptures the things concerning Himself" (vv. 25–27). As Jesus explained all the Scriptures written about Him, He made clear to these distraught disciples everything that had to take place to fulfill the prophecies concerning the Savior.

As the travelers approached the village, although they still did not recognize Him, they invited Jesus to stay, since it was toward evening and the cultural custom of hospitality required them to offer shelter for the night. So He went in with them, and later as they sat at the table to eat, He took bread, blessed it, broke it, and gave it to them, and their eyes were opened to recognize who He was. *They had been with Jesus!* Immediately, He disappeared from their sight.

Can you hear their next words, as they stared wide-eyed

at one another? Verse 32 records them for us: "Did not our hearts burn within us while He talked to us on the road, while He opened to us the Scriptures?" Their hearts were filled with joy and wonder on their journey as Jesus shared the full meaning of the Scriptures—the Good News! They rushed back to the other disciples in Jerusalem, exclaiming excitedly about everything that had happened to them, first on the road and then at the table.

Because they had been with Jesus, who revealed the Word to them, these disciples were changed! Soon, according to Luke, they would be "clothed with power from on high" (v. 49), preaching repentance and proclaiming the forgiveness of sins in Jesus' name. They could not keep it the Good News to themselves; they wanted to share it with the world!

Just as the first disciples had been with Jesus, we, too, have been with Jesus!

- When we have remembered our Baptism, when God claimed us as His own dear daughters in Christ, forgave our sins through Jesus' atoning work on the cross, and filled us with His faith-giving Spirit, we have been with Jesus!

- When we have sojourned into His holy and precious Word, sitting at His feet, listening to His perfect promise of salvation, and clinging to His every command, we have been with Jesus!

- When we have knelt at His Table to receive His body and blood, offering us refreshment and renewal in faith, we have been with Jesus!

• When we have lived in His continual presence, through the power and the work of the Holy Spirit, who enables us to live our lives for the Word made flesh, we have been with Jesus—and we have been changed!

As we spend time with Jesus, we are continuously changed. Our once-timid tootsies become bold and courageous. Our feet are unfastened from our comfort zone. The Holy Spirit propels us forward, enabling and empowering us to live life on the edge with Jesus! We step out, walking beside Him and learning from Him. He opens our eyes to see how He is at work and where He is at work, drawing people to Himself today. Being continuously transformed into His image by the power of the Spirit (see 2 Corinthians 3:18), we become more and more like Jesus in our daily walk with Him. Our desires and our dreams, our passions and our priorities, begin to line up with His.

Being with Jesus means living on the edge, because the edge is how He lived; the edge is where He lived during His earthly ministry.

How Did Jesus Live?

• Jesus lived life courageously, not intimidated by the threats of His adversaries and not afraid to go against the grain in order to proclaim the truth of God's love and forgiveness. "But woe to you, scribes and Pharisees, hypocrites!" Jesus warned in His seven woes recorded in Matthew 23 (v. 13). He boldly confronted the legalism and lies of the religious leaders that stood in direct opposition to God's grace and truth, even when doing so meant He would face persecution and death at the hands of those leaders.

- Jesus lived intentionally. Never sidetracked or distracted, His mission was clear, focused, and centered on God's purpose. As Jesus spoke of being the one true Shepherd of the sheep, He stated His mission and purpose: "I came that they may have life and have it abundantly" (John 10:10).

- Jesus lived compassionately. His heart was soft and tender for the hurting and the humble. He came to them with a message of mercy and with hands that healed. "When He saw the crowds, He had compassion for them, because they were harassed and helpless, like sheep without a shepherd" (Matthew 9:36).

- Jesus lived sacrificially. So great was His love for all humankind—for you and for me—that He willingly gave up His own life in order that ours might be spared. He said, "The good shepherd lays down His life for the sheep. . . . I lay down My life that I may take it up again. No one takes it from Me, but I lay it down of My own accord" (John 10:11, 17–18).

This is how Jesus, our Good Shepherd, our Lord and our Savior, lived life on the edge. And it is the life He calls us to live too.

- Being with Jesus, we are empowered to speak courageously in His name, unafraid of those who would oppose His work and His Word. Take, for example, one brave woman whose recent mission work enabled her to teach native English teachers in Tsunami-stricken Banda Aceh, Indonesia. Her work opened doors for conversation about Christ with these precious people living in a nation where Christianity is forbidden. This woman is living on the edge courageously!

- Being with Jesus, and by God's grace, we can live intentionally, being purposeful and deliberate in all that we say and do in our witness to Him. One amazing woman that I know sees every interaction as an opportunity to shine Christ's light and share His love. As she meets new people, she says, "How can I pray for you or your family today?" She is met with warm responses again and again as she walks in faith intentionally and doors are opened to her witness for Christ.

- Being with Jesus, we can live compassionately, showing and giving our concern and care to a world in need, by His power at work in us. This very compassion led a group of Christian volunteers to provide and serve breakfast to the schoolchildren of a poverty-stricken portion of their city. As these volunteers interact with the children, they have the opportunity to shine the Savior's light. They serve in the name of Jesus Christ and out of compassion for His people.

- Being with Jesus, we actually have the ability to love sacrificially in His name. This love prompted dear friends of mine to trade their security, their home, and their possessions for a humble dwelling in Papua New Guinea, to live among the native people and bring the saving love of Jesus to them. And thousands of other families and individuals have done similarly through long-term and short-term mission service or through active mission support. They have sacrificed their time, their resources, and their lives so that souls may be saved for Christ; they love others sacrificially as the Lord leads them.

Where Did Jesus Live?

- Jesus surrounded Himself first with His disciples, stepping into the lives of those whose hearts would be softened and molded for the same mission with the same passion for saving the lost. Recall, from the previous chapter, Christ's call to His first followers: "Follow Me, and I will make you become fishers of men" (Mark 1:17).

- Jesus placed Himself where there were needs, physical and spiritual. He stepped into the lives of the sick and the lame, the poor and the humble, the sinners and the outcasts. "And Jesus went throughout all the cities and villages, teaching in their synagogues and proclaiming the gospel of the kingdom and healing every disease and every affliction" (Matthew 9:35).

- Jesus went where there were ears that needed to hear the way of salvation: He taught, "I am the way, and the truth, and the life. No one comes to the Father except through Me" (John 14:6). Wherever He went, He stepped into the lives of the people in that region with a message of grace, the hope of eternal life in His name.

Where Can We Live?

- As followers of Jesus, living on the edge, we surround ourselves first with other disciples, those who share the same heart for the spread of the Gospel and the passion for reaching the lost for Christ through the church, in ministry, and in mission.

- As followers of Jesus, we place ourselves in a position to help meet the needs—physical and spiritual—of the hurting, the hungry, and the helpless. We do this right in our own communities and all around the world.

- As followers of Jesus, we go where the Lord leads, where there are ears to hear the Good News! We meet Jesus out on the edge, where He is already at work.

Each of us has the amazing privilege of living on the edge with Jesus, but for every one of us the edge looks different. No other life is uniquely like yours. By our Creator's design, no one else possesses the same gifts and talents, the same open doors and opportunities, the same set of priorities and passions as you.

Enter Their World

Bring the saving love of Christ with you as you make yourself available to others, as you enter their world:

- The world of the lonely neighbors next door or the family in another part of the country whose disaster-stricken city has left them homeless

- The world of the wayward teens in your local high school or the lost teens in India who have never heard the Gospel

- The world of the hungry children of your town or the villagers in Tanzania, Africa, who are hungry for a place to worship

Where lie your God-given gifts and passions to make a difference, to change someone's world for Christ?

How are you able to share His grace, demonstrate His love, and hand out hope in His name?

What needs trigger your passion to be actively involved in supporting mission outreach?

Whom is He placing in your path as you live out there on that edge, as you are called by God to give help in this life and hope for eternity?

In today's world of cynics and skeptics, doubters and disbelievers, to speak the truth of Jesus is really edgy living. But the Savior of all nations, the King of kings and the Lord of lords, has called you to enter their world. He is providing you with opportunities and open doors to speak courageously about the only way to salvation to a desperate world in need.

By the almighty power of the Spirit, you can obediently join Jesus out there on that edge, where He is already at work. He has chosen you. He has blessed you to be a blessing to others, to go, serve, and witness!

Look around at your sisters and brothers in Christ within your church, your ministry, and your community. They have been with Jesus. They are living on the edge too, right next to you. Edgy living, together in Christ! What can we do together?

- Together, we can feed those who are hungry in body and soul. We can provide help for the hurting and bring aid to the sick and the struggling, all in the name of Jesus.

- Together, we can educate people, providing means for their future. We can assist others in the church and in the mission field, in the name of Jesus.

- Together, we can share the one and only hope of salvation in Christ to a lost world in need of a Savior.

Yes, being with Jesus moves us to the edge. Are you on the edge of your seat, with bated breath, in anticipation of what He has in store for you? Like the disciples on the road to Emmaus, may our hearts burn within us as we hear the truth proclaimed. Fueled with the fire of the Holy Spirit, may we leap toward the edge with the love of Christ to a world that needs to hear His saving message, confident that He is right here beside us. Our firm foundation lives out here on the edge. We have been with Jesus too!

Reflections

1. In the previous chapters, we looked at many sins and struggles that could leave us trapped behind our imaginary diving board. As you look back to each chapter topic, which stood out to you as those you struggle with the most? Ask for the Spirit's strength to step out. Go to God's Word. Seek an accountability partner to encourage you and to pray for you or with you.

2. You have been with Jesus! How have you been changed as you spend time with Him? What have you learned from the Lord in your study of His Word lately?

3. Take a look at 2 Corinthians 3:18. How are you being transformed in His image?

4. Read Luke 24:13–35. As you do, slip your feet into the sad sandals of either grieving disciple. Not yet recognizing Jesus, but having just heard the Scriptures explained so clearly, the flicker of hope is growing in the disciple's heart; a flicker that bursts into full flame as he recognizes his risen Savior! Imagine that hope!

5. How have you seen others living on the edge? Courageously? Intentionally? Compassionately? Sacrificially? Think of specific examples. Share. How might you live on the edge, by the power of the Spirit?

6. Envision Christ extending His hand to you from the edge, calling you to step out beside Him and join Him where He is already at work. What does this edge look like? Consider your unique set of gifts and talents, your open doors and opportunities, your passions and priorities.

7. How can you make yourself available this week, entering someone's world so that you might share the saving love of Christ or encourage her in her faith walk? Review the questions under the "Enter Their World" section of this chapter.

8. Joining hands with your sisters and brothers in Christ, what, specifically, can you do together as you live on the edge for Christ? Develop a plan, knowing that your Savior is right here beside you.

Write further
reflections here